POSTER COLLECTION

ARMIN HOFMANN

07

Mit einem Essay von / Essay by Steven Heller

T0348996

MUSEUM FÜR GESTALTUNG ZÜRICH
PLAKATSAMMLUNG / POSTER COLLECTION

LARS MÜLLER PUBLISHERS

1 Henry Moore / Oskar Schlemmer
1955

VORWORT

Als Armin Hofmann 1963 ein Plakat für das Tellspiel vorlegte, brachte er in der typischen, klangvollen Ökonomie seiner Mittel zum Ausdruck, welch grundlegendem Wandel die angewandte Kunst unterworfen war. Das Tellspiel ist ein in der Schweizer Volkskultur fest verankerter Anlass, bei dem ein Laientheater das Epos des Nationalhelden Wilhelm Tell aufführt. Mit dem Apfel und dem Pfeil greift Hofmann zwar die unverzichtbaren Symbole der Tell-Legende auf, doch er verdichtet sie mittels Schrift und Bild zu einer zeichenhaften Abstraktion von einer Eleganz, die für die Thematik beispiellos war. In der Plakatgestaltung gab es wohl kaum eine Sphäre, die gegen eine zeitgemässe Sprache resistenter gewesen wäre als jene, in der die Schweizer Geschichte beschwört wurde. So mag man sich staunend fragen, wie Hofmann die Kunden von seiner Arbeit überzeugen konnte.

Seine Plakate sind visuelle Appelle, die über die primäre Information hinausweisen. Der rasche technologische und gesellschaftliche Wandel drängte ihn immer wieder zur ebenso scharfsinnigen wie diskreten Forderung nach einer gestalterischen Haltung, die einer modernen, vielschichtigen Gesellschaft eine adäquate visuelle Kultur zur Seite zu stellen vermag. Und «modern» heisst hier nicht nur im technologischen Sinn auf der Höhe der Zeit zu sein, sondern auch in der Lage, seine geistige und berufliche Beweglichkeit zu erhalten, raschen Umwälzungen mit Persönlichkeit und Intuition zu begegnen und Geschichte ohne Wehmut als Teil des Lebens anzunehmen.

Dass er solche Signale aus der Mitte eines Umkreises senden konnte, der den Traditionalisten vorenthalten schien, mag damit erklärt werden, dass er ein begnadeter Vermittler ist. Hofmann überzeugt, weil er keine Lehrmeinungen verbreitet, sondern persönliche Erfahrungen; Weil er gefühlsbetontes und rationales Vorgehen nicht als gegensätzlich empfindet; Weil er Gesetzmässigkeiten des Designs auch mit den Sinnen begreift. Hofmann verstand sein Werk und seine vierzig Jahre während Lehrtätigkeit an der Allgemeinen Gewerbeschule Basel als gleichwertig. Darum erfüllten seine Plakate auch einen didaktischen Zweck und verwandelten die Strassen der Stadt in ein offenes Klassenzimmer, in dem über Form und Wirkung debattiert wurde. Trotz ihrer lokalen Gebundenheit sind die Plakate zu Prototypen einer Haltung geworden, die nicht nur in der Schweiz, sondern namentlich in den USA, wo Hofmann regelmässig lehrte, für hunderte von Studierenden ausserordentlich folgenreich war.

Die Vorbereitungen zu diesem Band haben einmal mehr gezeigt, dass es noch keine verlässliche Geschichte des Schweizer Grafik Designs und seiner Ausstrahlung gibt. Wir sind daher besonders glücklich, bei Armin und Dorothea Hofmann und vielen ehemaligen Studierenden begeisterte Unterstützung erfahren zu haben beim Versuch zu differenzieren, was oft zu leichtfertig dem Schlagwort «Swiss Style» untergeordnet wird.

Felix Studinka

FOREWORD

When Armin Hofmann produced a poster for William Tell in 1963, he used the typically sonorous economy of his resources to show what a fundamental change applied art was undergoing. The Tell play is firmly established in popular Swiss culture as a way for amateur theatres to act out the epic of the national hero William Tell. Hofmann takes up the indispensable symbols of the Tell legend, the apple and the arrow, but uses typeface and image to condense them into a symbolic abstraction of an elegance unparalleled for this subject matter. There was probably no sphere of poster design that might have been more resistant to up-to-date language than the sphere of Swiss history. So we may be sufficiently surprised to wonder how Hofmann managed to persuade clients to accept his work.

His posters are visual appeals that point beyond the primary information. Rapid technological and social change constantly pushed him to make demands, as astute as they were discreet, for a design approach able to provide a visual culture appropriate to a modern, complex society. And here "modern" is to be understood not just as being state-of-the-art in the technological sense. It also implies being able to retain one's mental and professional agility, to confront ultra-rapid change with personality and intuition, and to accept history as a part of life, without wistful nostalgia.

His talents as a communicator could explain the fact that he was able to send signals of this kind from a circle that seemed to be reserved for traditionalists. Hofmann is convincing because he does not pass on educational opinions, but his own experience; because he does not see emotional and rational approaches as mutually exclusive; because he appreciates the inherent laws of design with his senses as well. Hofmann accorded equal value to his work and his forty years of teaching at the Allgemeine Gewerbeschule Basel. For this reason his posters also fulfilled a didactic purpose and transformed the streets of the city into an open classroom in which form and effect were debated. Despite being tied to a particular locality, the posters became prototypes for an attitude that made an extraordinary impact on hundreds of students not only in Switzerland, but also especially in the USA, where Hofmann taught regularly.

The preparations for this volume have again shown that there is still no reliable history of Swiss design and the effect it has had. We are therefore particularly pleased to have been supported so enthusiastically by Armin and Dorothea Hofmann and many former students in our efforts to delineate something that is often all too loosely placed under the heading "Swiss Style".

Felix Studinka

2 Robert Jacobsen / Serge Poliakoff
1958

3 **Stadtthater Basel 63/64**
1963

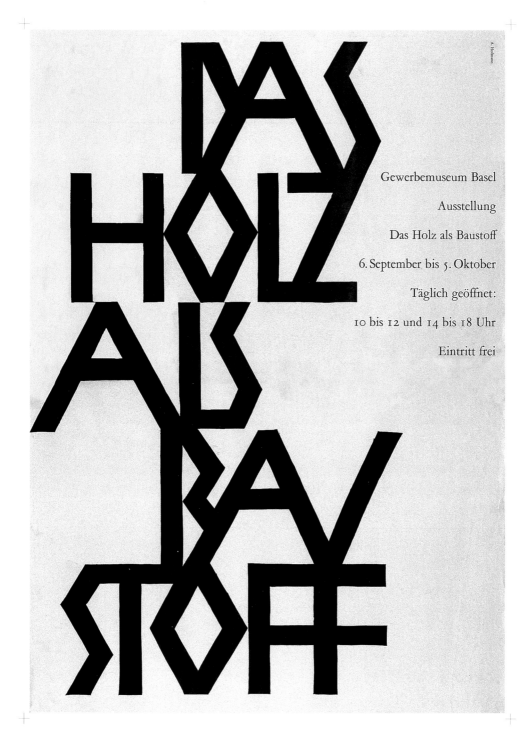

A. Hofmann

Gewerbemuseum Basel

Ausstellung

Das Holz als Baustoff

6. September bis 5. Oktober

Täglich geöffnet:

10 bis 12 und 14 bis 18 Uhr

Eintritt frei

4 **Das Holz als Baustoff**
Wood as a Building Material
1952

Basler Theater 1968/9

Entwurf: A.Holmann / Druck: Wassermann A.G.

5 **Basler Theater 1968/9**
1968

5.
Febr.
bis 13. März
**Kunsthalle
Basel
Graham
Sutherland
EL
Lissitzky**

6 Graham Sutherland/El Lissitzky
1966

Stadttheater

Basel

Während
der Saison
1960/61
finden Sie
an dieser
Stelle
den
Spielplan

7 **Stadttheater Basel 1960/61**
1960

ARMIN HOFMANNS GRAFISCHE SCHLAGKRAFT

Steven Heller

Jemand hat einmal erklärt, ein erfolgreiches Werbeplakat müsse aus einer Entfernung von dreissig Metern deutlich wahrzunehmen sein. Er wollte damit sagen, dass selbst ein Entwurf von exquisiter Schönheit wirkungslos bleibt, wenn das Plakat nicht auf den ersten Blick die Aufmerksamkeit eiliger Passanten auf sich ziehen kann. Das ganze 20. Jahrhundert hindurch hat man versucht, diesen Gedanken in die Tat umzusetzen, mit wechselnden Methoden: vom unzweideutigen Sachplakat der frühen 1900er bis hin zu den optisch provozierenden psychedelischen Plakaten der späten 1960er Jahre. Einige erreichen ihre Wirkung mit mehr, andere mit weniger visuellem Lärm, doch eines ist gewiss: Jedes Plakat braucht eine ganz andere grafische Schlagkraft als «intimere» Druckerzeugnisse. Am besten erlebbar (denn sie lässt sich tatsächlich eher emotional erleben als intellektuell erfassen) ist diese Schlagkraft für mich im Gesamtwerk des Schweizer Grafikers und Lehrers Armin Hofmann. Wie keine anderen überbrücken seine Plakate die Kluft zwischen Repräsentation und Abstraktion; kaum ein anderer Grafiker hat so viele Plakate geschaffen, die – ob aus einer Entfernung von dreissig Metern oder dreissig Zentimetern – einen derart lebendigen Eindruck auf den Betrachter machen.

In seiner sich über mehr als sechs Jahrzehnte erstreckenden Laufbahn hat Hofmann viele Plakat-Ikonen entworfen. Um nur einige wenige zu nennen: die Hände für das Stadttheater Basel 3, das riesige C für die Sammlung Cavellini 13, die sich spiralförmig windende Ballerina für Giselle 66 und der kühne Apfel für Wilhelm Tell 67. Sein bedeutendster und bekanntester Beitrag zur Geschichte des Plakats dürfte jedoch das von 1954 für eine Ausstellung in der Schweizer Mustermesse in Basel sein, das den treffenden Titel «Die gute Form» 27 trägt . Dieser rein typografische Entwurf ist zugleich konkret und abstrakt, einfach und komplex, konventionell und radikal. Es erfüllt alle Anforderungen, die an ein Plakat gestellt werden können: es zieht das Auge an, weckt die Neugier, übermittelt eine Botschaft – und es braucht dafür weder eine explizite bildliche Darstellung noch einen cleveren Slogan.

Der Schriftzug «Die gute Form» ist jedoch eigentlich ein Bild, und das Bild ist ein Schriftzug, der als Text oder als Symbol gelesen werden kann – oder mit einem Blick als sowohl das eine wie das andere. Um zu erreichen, dass das Plakat einen unauslöschlichen Eindruck hinterlässt, entwarf Hofmann geometrisch präzise, völlig neuartige Buchstabenformen, die derart harmonisch zu den drei Wörtern zusammengesetzt und dann teilweise verdeckt worden sind, dass sie ihre Lesbarkeit nicht einbüssen. Eine phänomenale Leistung. Dem Betrachter werden eine oder zwei Sekunden abverlangt, um den Schriftzug zu dekodieren, doch dann erschliessen sich ihm die geheimnisvolle Schönheit und die Bedeutung des Plakats.

Viel unbeholfener habe ich oben zu erklären versucht, was Hofmann so mühelos mit wenigen, taktisch meisterhaft gesetzten Zeichen auf Papier zu erreichen wusste!

Hofmann ist ein Meister der eloquenten Ökonomie, nicht des kalten stereotypen Reduktionismus, wie er mit der offiziösen (für Verpackungen, Strafzettel und Formulare verwendeten) Variante des Schweizer Stils in den 1950er und 1960er Jahren assoziiert wird, sondern einer anmutigen komplexen Simplizität, die rein ästhetische und ausgesprochen funktionale Werte miteinander verbindet. Zwar ist seine – aus radikalen (nie überflüssigen) Massstabswechseln, einem peniblen (nie vorhersagbaren) typografischen Arrangement und einem krassen (keineswegs klinischen) Symbolismus zusammengesetzte grafische Sprache in dem verwurzelt, was als «Schweizer Rationalismus» bezeichnet wird, doch sie ist von einem ganz persönlichen, gefühlsbetonten Dialekt durchdrungen. Häufig wird der orthodoxe Schweizer Grafikstil als kalt und formelhaft gescholten, doch Hofmann trotzt dieser Schmalspurigkeit und transzendiert sie.

«Die gute Form» ist auf einem starren Raster verankert, doch dank der energischen Flüssigkeit der Hofmannschen Typografie bleibt der Anker für das nackte Auge unsichtbar. Dasselbe gilt für seine anderen rein typografischen Plakate, deren «massgeschneiderte» Lettern mit ihrem skulpturalen Charakter sowohl konventionell gelesen als auch emotional erlebt werden können. «Tempel und Teehaus in Japan» (1955) 32, «Das Holz als Baustoff» (1952) 4 und «Karl Geiser» (1957) 31 haben mehr Persönlichkeit und mit ihren nur wenigen, raffiniert konstruierten, aufeinandergeschichteten und miteinander verbundenen Wörtern mehr mitzuteilen als die meisten Bilderzählungen. Wie mit «Die gute Form» hat Hofmann auch mit diesen Plakaten abstrakte Gebilde geschaffen, die auf den ersten Blick sowohl als Muster wie auch als Text erkennbar sind. Wenn mehrere Exemplare eines dieser Plakate in einer Reihe an einer Wand oder in einem Schaukasten zu sehen sind, nimmt der Betrachter die ästhetischen Qualitäten – ein dramatisches Formarrangement – wahr, doch wenn ein Plakat einzeln betrachtet wird, ist die Botschaft so deutlich zu lesen wie auf einem konventionellen Anschlag.

Die Dramatik, die Hofmann mit wenigen Wörtern erreichen kann, wird noch intensiver, wenn er nur mit zwei Buchstaben arbeitet. Eines seiner Leitmotive ist tatsächlich die kühne Kombination zweier Grossbuchstaben – modernistische Monogramme – für eine Folge von Plakaten für Ausstellungen in der Kunsthalle Basel. Alle diese Ausstellungen waren jeweils zwei Künstlern gewidmet, die – der eine ein Vertreter der Gegenständlichkeit, der andere einer der Abstraktion – auf den ersten Blick oft kaum zueinander passen wollten. Hofmann fügte für die Plakate die Initialen der Nachnamen zu gewaltigen Monogrammen zusammen, zum Beispiel «CL» 21 für Fernand Léger und Alexander Calder (1957), «SJ» 17 für David Smith und Horst Janssen (1966) und «KJ» 26 für Franz Kline und Alfred Jensen (1964). Das Monogramm-Motiv ist eine elegante Idee, die das traditionelle Kunstplakat in ein linguistisches Spiel verwandelt. Statt zwei repräsentative Werke der beiden Künstler aufeinander prallen zu lassen, macht Hofmann deren Initialen zu einem «Markenzeichen», das nicht nur die Ausstellung kennzeichnet, sondern den Betrachter in ein Entzifferungsspiel hineinzwingt. So erstaunlich diese Zusammenstellungen waren, so erstaunlich waren Hofmanns Lösungen. Das wiederum kann gar nicht erstaunen.

Hofmanns Werk kennt keine Routine. Zwar gibt es, wenn man sein Gesamtwerk betrachtet, zwangsläufige Konsistenzen, die seinen Stil erkennen lassen, doch nichts in seinem Œuvre ist konventionell, und ganz gewiss nicht in den frühen 1950er Jahren, als seine ersten charakteristischen Entwürfe entstanden. Nichts könnte diese Behauptung besser stützen als seine gesammelten Theaterplakate für das Stadttheater Basel, dem Hofmann in den späten 1950er und in den 1960er Jahren eine unverwechselbare Identität gab. Es sind keine typischen, mit «Lockvögeln» oder Namenslisten überladenen Theaterplakate, noch sensationelle oder romantische Abbildungen als Kostproben aus dem Repertoire. Hofmanns Theaterplakate sind symbolische Zusammenfassungen und ikonische Interventionen, die dem Publikum das Sprech- und Musiktheaterangebot vorstellen und zugleich eine visuelle Herausforderung bieten. Statt dem Publikum nur die Fakten mitzuteilen, stellen sie ihm die Aufgabe, die Bedeutung der Bilder zu interpretieren. Zwar wird dem Betrachter kein schwieriges Quiz präsentiert, doch Bilder wie ein riesiges Ohr und Auge (für die Spielzeit 1962/63) 52, ein lachender Clown (für die Spielzeit 1960/61) 7 oder ein finsteres/manisches Gesicht (für das Plakat von 1967) 59 verlangen von ihm, sich auf die visuellen Reize einzulassen und kein passiver Rezipient zu bleiben.

Sowenig Hofmann dem Betrachter Passivität zugesteht, sowenig ist sie Teil seines visuellen Vokabulars. Man braucht sich nur seine zum Klassiker gewordene *Methodik der Form- und Bildgestaltung* (Teufen, 1965) anzuschauen (und später natürlich zu lesen), um zu verstehen, dass Hofmanns Entwürfe zielbewusst animiert sind, damit das Auge des Betrachters verschiedenen Wegen folgt, die er durch sein grafisches und typografisches Feld gezogen hat. Ich habe immer den Eindruck gehabt, dass sein im übrigen statisches Werk für die Leinwand oder den Bildschirm genauso geeignet ist wie für das Papier, und ich wage die Behauptung, dass er sich wahrscheinlich, wenn er denn heute noch einmal von vorn anfangen könnte, hauptsächlich mit bewegten Bildern beschäftigen würde. Sollten Sie daran zweifeln, dass Hofmanns statische Bilder – nicht wild, sondern schlüssig – um einen mentalen Bildschirm herumspringen, brauchen Sie die Augen nur über die in seinem Handbuch abgebildeten Reihen geometrischer Layout-Optionen wandern zu lassen. Und wenn Sie sich dann seine an einer Wand aneinandergereihten Plakate vorstellen (vor allem die für das Gewerbemuseum Basel) oder die Seiten dieses Buches umschlagen, werden Sie sich der ungehemmten kinetischen Energie und kinematografischen Kraft nicht entziehen können.

Fast sein ganzes Leben lang hat Hofmann als Grafiker und Typograf für Printmedien gearbeitet, und deshalb würde er selbst sein Werk wohl kaum unter filmischen Gesichtspunkten beschreiben wollen. Es ist jedoch unverkennbar, dass seine ausgeprägte kinetische Sensibilität in Plakate eingegangen ist, die die starren Grenzen des Mediums überschreiten. Und das ist auch das Kennzeichen, das sein Werk so unmissverständlich modern macht.

«Modernismus» ist natürlich ein unpräziser Begriff, der die radikale Revision künstlerischer Standards durch Avantgardekünstler in der Mitte des 20. Jahrhunderts bezeichnet, und Hofmann wurde zweifellos von den grossen Avantgardisten seiner Zeit beeinflusst. Wie der seines Freundes Paul Rand ist jedoch auch Hofmanns Modernismus eine durch und durch persönliche Interpretation, die sich nicht auf die ideologischen Requisiten der Schlüsselbewegungen und -schulen beschränkt. Rand war für seinen verspielten Humor bekannt, der sich zu den Comicstrips und Schaufensterplakaten, die in seiner Jugend in Brooklyn, New York, sowohl einen positiven als auch einen negativen Einfluss auf ihn ausgeübt hatten, ebenso ironisch bekannte wie zu den formalen und inhaltlichen Vorstellungen der Dada- und der Bauhaus-Bewegung, die er später kennen lernte. Hofmann wurde 1920 in Winterthur geboren und studierte zunächst in Zürich, in einer anderen ästhetischen und philosophischen Umgebung als Rand. Obwohl er nicht genau denselben Einflüssen ausgesetzt war, war (und ist) sein dem europäischen Modernismus verpflichteter spielerischer Instinkt kein bisschen weniger ausgeprägt, auch wenn ihm etwas Verhaltenes eigen ist, was sich in seiner Farbpalette zeigt, die sich fast immer auf Schwarz und Weiss oder Rot und Weiss beschränkt.

In seinen phantastisch verspielten und verspielt ernsthaften Plakaten – der Plakatfolge für das Gewerbemuseum Basel und einem Plakat für die «Herman Miller Collection» (1962) 46 – bedient er sich der Abstraktion so, wie Jackson Pollock Farbe tropfen liess: expressiv. Hofmanns amorphe Formen und dichte Farbfelder zittern und wackeln, stossen und parieren, drängen vor und weichen zurück in einer Art expressionistischer Improvisation. Die Schrift Univers ist jedoch ein Anker der Kon sistenz, der diese Plakate vor zu viel Anarchie bewahrt. Mit ihrer formalen Freiheit kommen diese Plakate meines Erachtens einem unabhängigen Ausdrucksgenre – weder schöne noch angewandte Kunst – nahe wie keine anderen. Eine Theorie, die, wie ich vermute, Hofmann – der sich durch und durch als Gebrauchsgrafiker versteht – von sich weisen dürfte.

In ihrer Gesamtheit verkörpern Hofmanns Plakate den Modernismus der Mitte des 20. Jahrhunderts, nicht, weil das Ornament verworfen wird und mechanische Methoden (d.h. Fotografien) an die Stelle handgezeichneter Dekorationen oder Illustrationen treten, sondern weil sie die Seele ihrer Zeit berühren. Ich weiss, dass es wohl nicht einfach ist, grosse Schriftzeichen in Schwarz und Weiss und manchmal in Rot oder kühne Geometrien oder scharfe Fotografien anzuschauen und dann das Wort «Seele» zu beschwören. Mir ist bewusst, dass Hofmanns Werk besser als eine Art wohlgeordnete klinische Schönheit charakterisiert werden könnte, doch in den Plakaten für das Stadttheater Basel (1955) 43, und für das Deutsche Requiem von Brahms 57 (1986) ist auch etwas so unglaublich Seelenvolles, dass es schwer fällt, dieses Wort nicht zu verwenden oder nicht entsprechend bewegt zu sein. Ich staune über die formale Reinheit dieser Plakate, spüre aber auch die Leidenschaft des Gestalters für das Material. Und obwohl er als Verfasser von Handbüchern und Lehrer an der Allgemeinen Gewerbeschule Basel und an der Yale University Standards und Formeln für die grafische Gestaltung etablierte, scheinen die Arbeiten seiner begabtesten Schüler deutlich zu zeigen, dass er nicht einfach nur das Evangelium der Standardisierung als Katechismus für jedes grafische Design predigte. Er gab seinen Schülern Werkzeuge an die Hand, mit denen – und ein festes Fundament, auf dem – sie klassische oder «zeitlose» Typografien errichten konnten, doch er vermittelte ihnen auch einen Sinn für Leidenschaft (oder Seele). Ohne eine restlose Hingabe an seine Kunst und Gestaltung hätte Hofmann die in dieser Sammlung zu findenden Werke nicht hervorbringen können: Plakate, die nicht nur in formaler Hinsicht der Zeit standhalten, sondern Betrachter wie zum Beispiel mich auch nach Jahren noch auf einer emotionalen Ebene ansprechen. Zusätzlich zu seiner meisterhaften Fähigkeit, Schrift und Bild zu handhaben, ist es diese Seele, die seinem Werk und seinem Erbe diese aussergewöhnliche Schlagkraft gibt.

**Rothko
Chillida**

3. III – 8. IV
Kunsthalle
Basel
Mark
Rothko
Eduardo
Chillida

8 Mark Rothko/Eduardo Chillida
1962

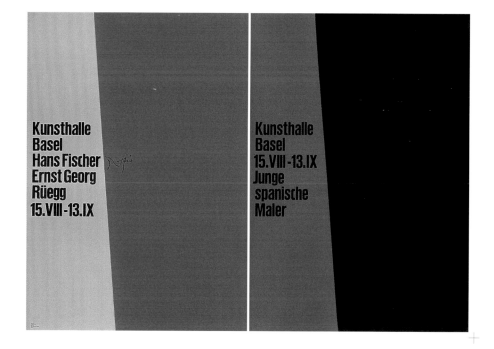

9 René Auberjonois/Ernest Bolens
1961

10 Hans Fischer/Ernst Georg Rüegg
1959

11 Paul Burckhardt/Emil Schill/Carlo König
1961

12 Junge spanische Maler
Young Spanish Painters
1959

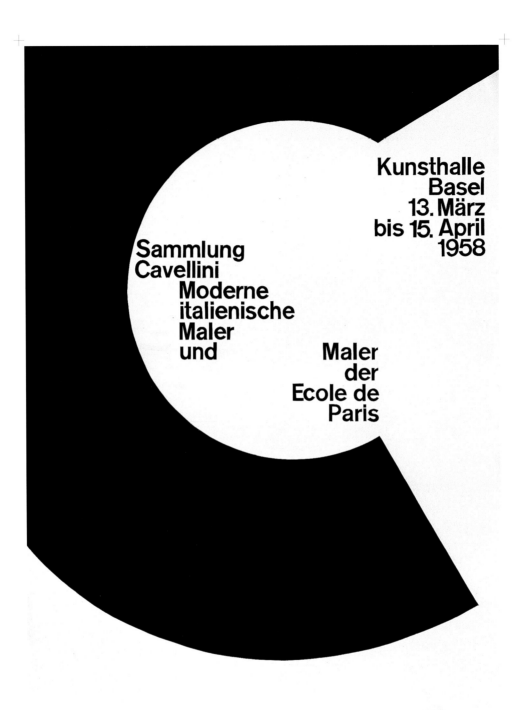

Sammlung
Cavellini
Moderne
italienische
Maler
und

Maler
der
Ecole de
Paris

Kunsthalle
Basel
13. März
bis 15. April
1958

13 Sammlung Cavellini
Cavellini Collection
1958

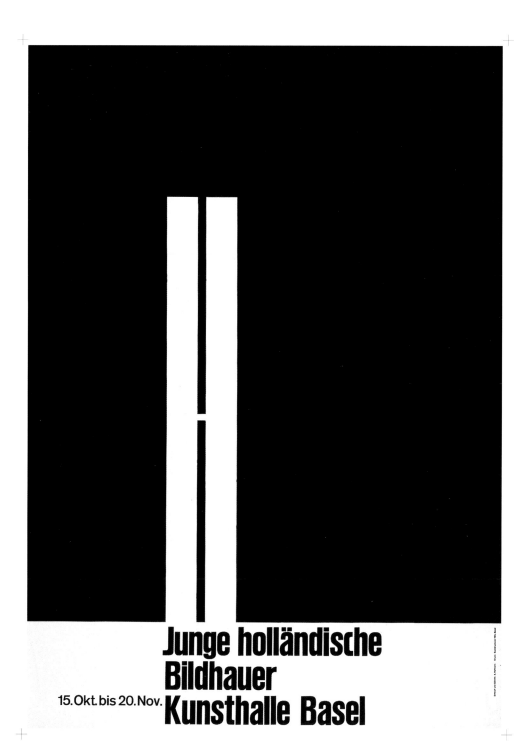

14 Junge holländische Bildhauer
Young Dutch Sculptors
1960

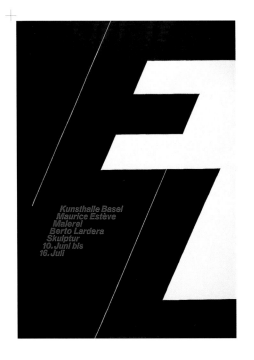

Kunsthalle Basel
Maurice Estève
Malerei
Berto Lardera
Skulptur
10. Juni bis
16. Juli

25. Okt.
bis
23. Nov.

Kunsthalle
Basel
David SMITH
Skulpturen
Horst
JANSSEN
Zeichnungen
Graphik

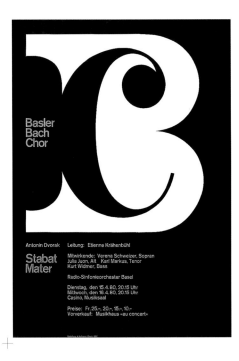

Basler
Bach
Chor

Antonin Dvorak   Leitung: Etienne Krähenbühl

Stabat
Mater

Mitwirkende: Verena Schweizer, Sopran
Julia Juon, Alt   Karl Markus, Tenor
Kurt Widmer, Bass

Radio-Sinfonieorchester Basel

Dienstag, den 15.4.80, 20.15 Uhr
Mittwoch, den 16.4.80, 20.15 Uhr
Casino, Musiksaal

Preise: Fr. 25.–, 20.–, 15.–, 10.–
Vorverkauf: Musikhaus «au concert»

Kunst II.6 Deutsche
halle bis Künstler der
Basel 12.7 Gegenwart

15 Maurice Estève/Berto Lardera
1961

16 Basler Bach Chor
Basel Bach Choir
1980

17 David Smith/Horst Janssen
1966

18 Deutsche Künstler der Gegenwart
Contemporary German Artists
1959

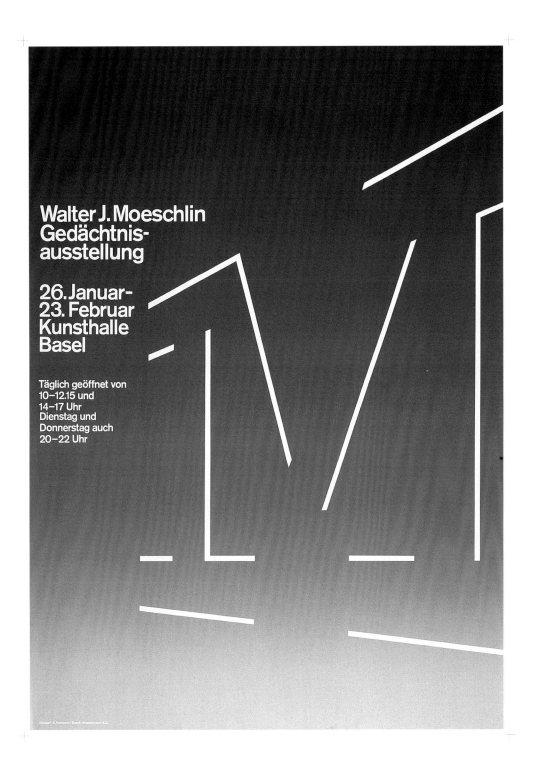

19 Walter J. Moeschlin
1969

20 **Willi Baumeister/Ernst Wilhelm Nay**
1960

Kunsthalle
Basel
Fernand
Léger
Alexander
Calder
22. Mai bis
23.   Juni

21 Fernand Léger/Alexander Calder
1957

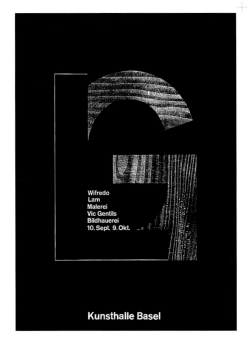

22 Junge Berliner Künstler
Young Berlin Artists
1966

23 Ernst Morgenthaler
1962

24 Wilfredo Lam/Vic Gentils
1966

25 Phillip Martin/Ennio Morlotti/Hans R. Schiess
1967

Franz
Kline
Alfred Jensen
Kunsthalle
Basel
31. Januar
1. März

26 **Franz Kline / Alfred Jensen**
1964

ARMIN HOFMANN'S GRAPHIC IMPACT

By Steven Heller

Someone once decreed that a successful advertising poster must be clearly viewed from a distance of one hundred feet, suggesting that if such a prominent image cannot instantaneously attract the attention of hurried passersby then even an exquisitely beautiful design is ineffectual publicity. This idea has been tested throughout the twentieth century with methods ranging from unambiguous Sachplakat (object poster) in the early 1900s to optically challenging psychedelic posters in the late 1960s. Some are effective with more and others with less visual noise, but one thing is certain every poster must have the kind of graphic impact that more intimate printed materials do not. For me this impact is best experienced (for it is indeed a visceral experience more than an intellectual one) in the collected work of Swiss graphic designer and teacher Armin Hofmann. His posters have uniquely bridged the divide between representation and abstraction, and in so doing few other designers' have produced more vivid work that can be seen from one hundred feet or one foot away.

Hofmann has created a great many poster icons over a six-decade-long career. These include but are not limited to the multiple hands for the Municipal Theater Basle 3, the huge C for the Cavellini Collection 13, the spiraling ballerina for Giselle 66, and the bold apple for William Tell 67. However, the appropriately titled "Die gute Form" (Good Design) 27, for a 1954 exhibition at the Swiss Industries Fair in Basle, is perhaps the designer's quintessential contribution to the poster field. This stark typographic design is at once concrete and abstract, simple and complex, conventional and radical. It does everything a poster should do – attract the eye, pique curiosity, impart a message – all, incidentally, without benefit of an explicit picture or clever slogan.

Yet the headline "Die gute Form" is, in fact, a picture and the picture is a headline that can be read either as words or symbols – or both at a single glance. To make this poster indelible Hofmann designed geometrically precise yet thoroughly novel letterforms that are so harmonious when composed into the three words and then partially obliterated, that they phenomenally retain their readability. The viewer is indeed asked to take a second or two to decode the lettering but once accomplished the mysterious beauty and overt significance of the poster is obvious.

I have used many more clumsy words in descriptive sentences in the above paragraph to explain what Hofmann so effortlessly achieved with just a few strategic marks on paper, which just goes to underscore the very essence of his achievement.

Hofmann is master of eloquent economy, not the cold stereotypical reductionism associated with the fifties- and sixties-era corporate variation of The Swiss Style (that is used on generic packages, traffic tickets, and business forms), but rather a graceful complex simplicity that combines purely aesthetic and distinctly functional values. While his graphic language, comprised of radical shifts in scale (never super-fluous), precisionist type arrangement (at no time predictable), and stark symbol-ism (by no means clinical), is rooted in what is referred to as Swiss rationalism it is nonetheless imbued with a particular personal dialect underscored by emotion. I have often heard critics of orthodox Swiss design who call it unrepentantly cold and formulaic, but Hofmann both defies and transcends this tunnel view.

"Die gute Form" is anchored on a rigid grid yet the armature is invisible to the naked eye thanks to the resolute fluidity of Hofmann's typography. The same is true with his other purely typographical posters wherein custom designed letterforms are constructed with sculptural character to be both conventionally read and intimately experienced. "Temple and Tea House in Japan" (1955) 32, "Wood as Building Material" (1952) 4, and "Karl Geiser" (1957) 31 have more personality, and actually tell more story with only a few smartly stacked, constructed, and interconnected words than most pictorial narratives. As with "Die gute Form", Hofmann has produced in these posters abstract entities that are immediately recognizable as both pattern and word. When each individual poster is viewed in a repeating sequence on a wall or display case the viewer experiences the aesthetic virtues – a dramatic arrangement of form – but when viewed individually the message is clearly readable as a conven-tional missive.

The drama Hofmann could achieve with just a few words is even more intense when he uses only two letters. Indeed one of Hofmann's recurring leitmotifs is the employ of two bold capitals – a modernist monogram – for a series of art exhibition posters at the Kunsthalle Basel. Each exhibition features two curiously and sometimes har-moniously matched artists and so for the poster Hofmann has two immense initials sharing the same bill, such as "CL" 21 for Fernand Léger and Alexander Calder (1957), "SJ" 17 for David Smith and Horst Janssen (1966) and "KJ" 26 for Franz Kline and Alfred Jensen (1964). The monogram motif is an elegant idea that transforms the traditional art poster into a kind of linguistic game. For rather than predictably reproduce two representative pieces of the artists' art resulting in a clash of styles, Hofmann makes the initials of the two exhibited artists into a trademark that not only "brands" the exhibit but forces the viewer to play along in a sport of deciphering. Since these curatorial pairings of representation and abstraction are surprising Hof-mann's solutions were surprising too. Which, actually, is not very surprising.

Hofmann's work repudiates routine. Although when seen as an entire body there are the inevitable consistencies that reveal Hofmann's style, but nothing in his oeuvre, certainly at the time he began his string of emblematic designs in the early 1950s, was anything customary. Indeed nothing supports this claim better than his collected theater posters for Stadt Theater Basel, to which the designer gave an indelible identity during the late 1950s and 1960s. These are not the typical theater bills laden with titillating teasers or obligatory credits, nor are they sensational or romantic depictions of the company's theatrical offerings. Hofmann's posters are symbolic summations and iconic interventions that serve to introduce the audience to dramatic or musical fare while offering a visual challenge. Rather than give only the facts these posters require that the audience interpret the meanings of the images. It is not a complicated quiz, but the questions posed by such pictures as a huge ear and eye (for the 1962/63 season) 52, a laughing clown (for the 1960/61 season) 7, or a scowling/maniacal face (for the 1967 poster) 59 demand that the audience interact with the stimuli rather than remain passive receivers.

Passivity is not what Hofmann demands of his viewer nor is it part of his own visual vocabulary. One need only to look at (and later read, of course) his classic *Graphic Design Manual* (Teufen, 1965) to understand that Hofmann's design is purposefully animated requiring that the viewer's eye navigate various pathways that he's carved through his field of type and image. I've always felt that his otherwise static work is equally suited to paper or screen, and I venture that if he were starting his career over again today motion might very well be his key occupation. If there is any doubt that Hofmann's static imagery is not jumping madly – though logically – around a mental screen simply scan the multiple rows of geometric layout options reproduced in his handbook. Then look at his posters together on a wall or turn the pages of this book (and particularly the posters for Gewerbemuseum Basel) to experience unbridled kinetic energy and cinematic power.

Hofmann has designed type and image for the print medium during the better part of his life, so naturally the relationship to film may not be exactly how he would chose to describe his work. But it is nonetheless clear that a distinct kinetic sensibility has contributed to making posters that transcend the inert confines of the medium. It is also the trait that makes his work so unequivocally modern.

Of course Modernism is an imprecise term that connotes the radical overhaul of artistic standards by mid-twentieth century avant-garde artists, and Hofmann is certainly influenced by the great advances of this time. Yet Hofmann's modernism, like his friend Paul Rand's, is a uniquely personal interpretation that reflects more than the ideological requisites of the key movements and schools. Rand was known for playful humor that ironically acknowledged the comic strips and show-card advertisements that were positive and negative influences on him while growing up in Brooklyn, New York, as well as the imported Dada and Bauhaus notions of form and content to which he was later exposed. Hofmann, born in Winterhur, Switzerland, in 1920, studied graphic art in a different aesthetic and philosophical environment in

Zurich and did not have the exact same influences as Rand, yet the play instinct bound to European Modernism was (and is) every bit as a intense. Nonetheless, unlike Rand, there is a hushed quality to Hofmann's play as evidenced in his color palette, which rarely changes from black and white or red and white.

His most stunningly playful and playfully serious series of posters for the Gewerbemuseum Basel and one for The Herman Miller Collection (1962) 46 use abstraction in the same way that Jackson Pollack dripped paint – expressively. Hofmann's amorphous shapes and solid color fields shake and wiggle, thrust and parry, lunge and recede in a kind of expressionistic improvisation. The Univers type, however, is an anchor of consistency that keeps these posters from being too anarchic. And yet I see these as free-form posters like no others that come close to being an independent genre of expression – neither fine nor applied art – a theory I suspect that Hofmann, the quintessential applied artist, might reject

Hofmann's posters collectively epitomize mid-century Modernism not because ornament is rejected and mechanical methods (i.e. photographs) are used in place of hand-drawn decoration or illustration, but because they touch the soul of their times. I know that it is probably difficult to look at large typefaces in black and white and sometimes red, or bold geometries, or crisp photographs and then conjure the word "soul." I realize that Hofmann's work might better be characterized as a kind of well-ordered clinical beauty, but there is also something so incredibly soulful in the posters for Stadt Theater Basle (1955) 43 and Brahms Requiem (1986) 57 that it is hard not to use the word or be accordingly moved. I marvel at their formal purity yet also feel the designer's passion for the material. And although as a writer of manuals and teacher at Basle School of Design and Yale University Hofmann established standards and formulae for design it seems apparent from the work of his most able students that he did not simply preach the gospel of standardization as a catechism for all design. He gave his students tools with which – and a solid armature on which – to build classical or "timeless" typography, but he also imparted a sense of passion (or soul). Hofmann could not produce the work found in this collection – posters that not only formally stand the test of time but continue to resonate with viewers such as myself on an emotional level – without a total commitment to his art and design. So in addition to his expert ability to manipulate type and image this soul is what gives this work and his legacy its impact.

27 **Die gute Form – Good Design**
1954

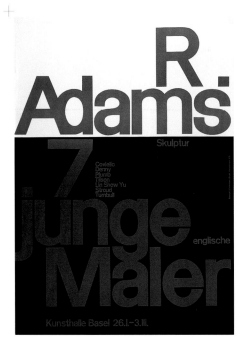

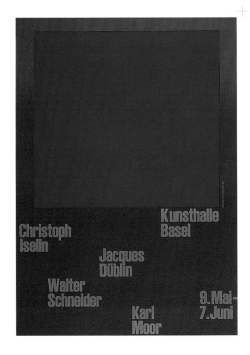

28 R. Adams/7 junge englische Maler
R. Adams/7 young English Painters
1963

29 Aeschbacher/Bill/Müller/Linck/4 Bildhauer
Aeschbacher/Bill/Müller/Linck/4 Sculptors
1959

30 Christoph Iselin/Walter Schneider/
Jacques Düblin/Karl Moor
1964

31 Karl Geiser
1957

TEMPEL und
TEE-
HAUS
in JAPAN

Tempel und Teehaus
in Japan
Ausstellung im
Gewerbemuseum
Basel
täglich geöffnet
4. Mai bis 31. Mai
10-12 und 14-18 Uhr
Eintritt frei

32 Tempel und Teehaus in Japan
Temple and Teahouse in Japan
1955

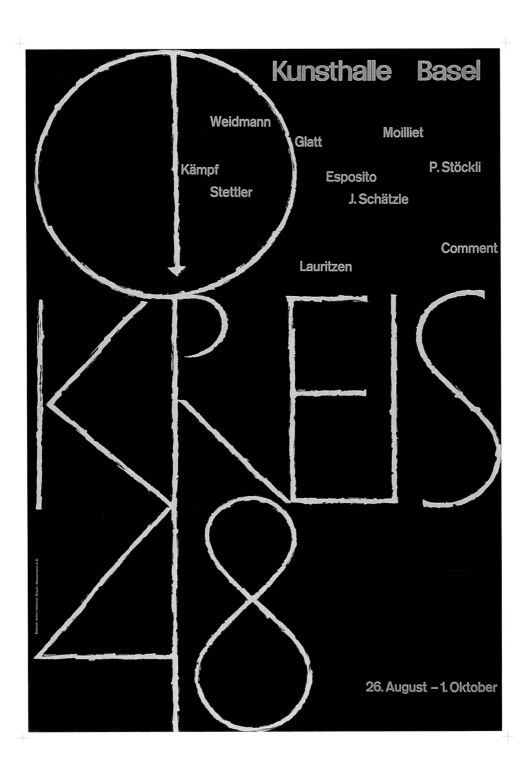

33 **Kreis 48**
1950

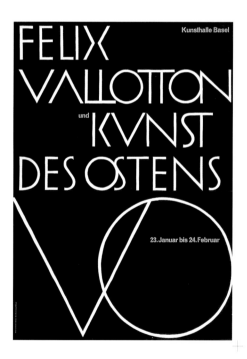

34 Walter Bodmer/Otto Tschumi/Teruko Yokoi
1964

35 Heinrich Müller/Marguerite Ammann/
Walter J. Moeschlin
1957

36 Moderne Malerei seit 1945 aus der Sammlung
Dotremont – Modern Painting since 1945 from the
Dotremont Collection
1961

37 Felix Vallotton und Kunst des Ostens
Felix Vallotton and the Art of the East
1957

38 **Die Schweiz zur Römerzeit**
Switzerland in Roman Times
1957

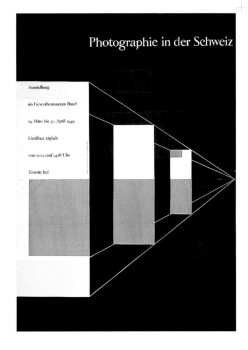

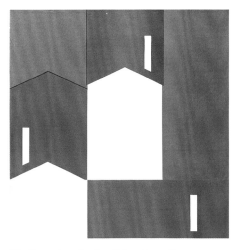

39 Münster-Scheiben-Entwürfe und Glasbilder von
Charles Hindenlang im Gewerbemuseum Basel
Minster Pane Designs and Stained Glass by Charles
Hindenlang in the Gewerbemuseum Basel
1952

40 Photographie in der Schweiz
Photography in Switzerland
1949

41 Siedlungsbau in der Schweiz 1938–47
Housing Estate Construction in Switzerland 1938–47
1948

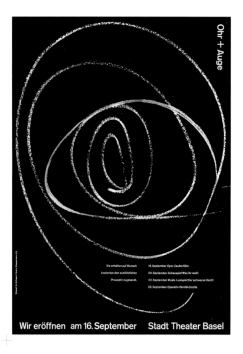

42 Rheinau-Initiative Ja
Rheinau Yes Initiative
1954

43 Ohr + Auge / Wir eröffnen am 16. September
Ear + Eye / We open on 16 September
1955

44 Theaterbau von der Antike bis zur Moderne
Theatre Construction in Antiquity and Modernity
1955

45 Basel und die Stadtstrassen der Zukunft
Basel and the Urban Roads of the Future
1961

Herman
Miller
Collection

Verkauf ab
9. März
Contura SA
Basel
Aeschen
vorstadt 4
Passage

Möbel unserer Zeit

46 Herman Miller Collection / Möbel unserer Zeit
Herman Miller Collection / Furniture of our Times
1962

5. Sept. bis
11. Okt.
Gewerbemuseum
Basel

Alte und
neue Formen
in Japan

47 Alte und neue Formen in Japan
Old and New Forms in Japan
1959

Luzern im Februar 2003
Felix Studinka

1937 und 1938 belegten Sie Kurse an der Kunstgewerbeschule Zürich. Welche Erwartungen hatten Sie an
die Schule?
**Ich wollte meine zeichnerische Begabung an der
Schule vertiefen.**

Wer waren Ihre Mentoren und was haben Sie von ihnen
gelernt?
**Sämtliche Lehrer haben mich beeindruckt: Heinrich
Müller, Walter Roshard, der Plastiker Fischer,
später auch Alfred Willimann und Ernst Keller, am
meisten jedoch Ernst Gubler.[1] Es war nicht der Stil
ihrer Arbeiten, sondern ihre Persönlichkeiten,
die mich beeindruckt haben, die Ernsthaftigkeit und
die Haltung, die ihrer Arbeit einen Inhalt gab.**

Inwieweit haben Sie damals die Verbreitung konstruktiver
Konzepte für die Gebrauchsgrafik wahrgenommen?
**Ich habe sie gar nicht wahrgenommen. Die ganze
Gruppe um Max Bill, Richard Paul Lohse,
Camille Graeser usw. war mir damals kein Begriff.**

1947 erhielten Sie, mit 27 Jahren und aus Zürich
kommend, erstmals ein festes Pensum an der Allgemein-
en Gewerbeschule Basel. Zwei Jahre zuvor hatte
Donald Brun[2], der ganz der illustrativen Tradition Basels
und dem Gewerbe verpflichtet war, seinen Unterricht
aufgenommen. Sollten Sie als jugendlicher Aussen-
seiter die «Moderne» verkörpern?
**Nein, das war ein reiner Zufall. Ich arbeitete damals
bei Fritz Bühler. Im Zug nach Zürich bin ich einmal
Ruder[3] begegnet. Ich las ein Büchlein über van Gogh
und so sind wir ins Gespräch gekommen. Er sagte,
dass sie einen Lehrer suchen würden und dass ich
mich in der Schule melden solle.
Später rief mir der Direktor der Schule von Grünigen[4]
an, weil er mich als Assistenten von Brun einstellen
wollte. Von Grünigen war während der Lithographen-
lehre in Zürich mein Lehrer gewesen. Ich bin nicht
als Neuerer eingestiegen, das war ganz anders. Ich
bin langsam in die Situation hinein gewachsen.**

Haben Sie auf diesem Weg festgestellt, dass Sie eine
pädagogische Begabung haben?
**Ich habe gespürt, dass die Schüler Grundlagen
brauchten. Als ich später neben Brun einen Kurs
übernahm, begann ich mit dem Versuch, Grundlagen
zu vermitteln und da hat von Grünigen festgestellt,
dass dies zu einem idealen Dialog gestalterischer
Auseinandersetzung führen könnte. Und Brun, der
menschlich wertvoll war, hat mir keine Steine**
in den Weg gelegt. Scheinbar war ich ein Pädagoge,
ohne es gewusst zu haben. Ich hatte ja noch keine
Erfahrung.

Zu welchem Zeitpunkt war Ihnen bewusst geworden,
dass Sie eine eigene Methode entwickelt haben?
**Das kam ganz langsam. Ich versuchte Einfachheit in
ihrer Kompliziertheit verständlich und praktisch
zu vermitteln, indem ich zu einem intensiven Studium
elementarer geometrischer Elemente wie etwa dem
Punkt oder der Linie anleitete, um ihre tieferen
Zusammenhänge in der Formenentwicklung erfahrbar
zu machen. Indem man etwas einfach gemacht hat,
ist es komplex geworden. Die Reduktion zu einer
Einfachheit hat Wissen und Gefühl erfordert. Es war
keine Methode, es war eine Haltung. Daraus ist
allmählich ein Konzept für den Unterricht entstanden
und die Schüler haben das mit Interesse aufgenommen.**

Was hat Ihren Unterricht international so begehrt
gemacht?
**Genau das: Die sichtbare Verbindung von Grund-
ausbildung und Anwendung machte den Unterricht
gefragt.**

Begriffe wie Sauberkeit, Einfachheit oder Konzentration
spielten bei Ihrer Erziehung eine grosse Rolle. Bezogen
sich solche Ideale auch auf die Förderung einer geistigen
Haltung?
**Ja, vor allem. Durch den Prozess entsteht eine
geistige Haltung.**

Ihr Unterricht war sehr viel umfassender als man
gemeinhin von dieser Ausbildung erwartete.
**Natürlich. Was ich vermitteln wollte, war nicht in
erster Linie Werbung, sondern ein Studium an
der Bilderwelt.**

Sie verbanden den Anspruch modern zu sein auch mit
einem ethischen Anspruch. Das erinnert an den
Ulmer Geist. Gab es Verbindungen zur Hochschule für
Gestaltung Ulm?
**Nein, es gab keine Verbindungen. Ulm nahm die
Basler Ausbildung kaum zur Kenntnis, da sie
den Hochschulstatus nicht besass. Basel war eine
Berufsschule, die ihrer eigenen Ethik folgte.**

Sie sind Zeuge einer unglaublichen technologischen
Entwicklung von der Lithografie bis zum Computer.
Welche Konsequenzen hatte diese Entwicklung für Ihren
Unterricht? Wie haben Sie Ihre Studierenden auf solche
Herausforderungen vorbereitet?
**Eher ins Gegenteil als man denken würde. Es ist
mir immer klarer geworden, dass Grundlagen
wichtiger werden. Je technischer die Welt, je unter-
teilter die Systeme, desto wichtiger wird die**

Vermittlung von Grundlagen. Darum habe ich versucht, Aufgabentypen als ganzheitliche Prozesse zu entwickeln: von der Vorstellung über die Skizze zum Entwurf bis zur Realisierung. Damit der Prozess sichtbar wird. Ich habe gesehen, dass es verhängnisvoll ist, wenn in den Schulen die Kopierapparate herumstehen, wo jeder Unsinn sofort kopiert und hundert Mal variiert wird und am Schluss liegen zahllose Versuche da und niemand weiss eigentlich was passiert ist. Mir ist lieber wenn jemand hundert Mal mit dem Bleistift seine eigene Arbeit überarbeitet und zu einer Erkenntnis kommt. Gerade der Linie, die mir vom zeichnerischen her viel bedeutete, habe ich meine besondere Aufmerksamkeit geschenkt, weil hier fast unbemerkt ein Element auftritt, das in der Geschichte der Menschen, sei es in der Natur, der Architektur, der Malerei, der Schrift oder in den Gegenständen des täglichen Lebens, eine exemplarische Bedeutung erhält.

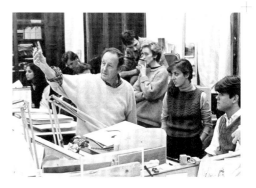

Sie haben immer wieder auf die Bedeutung der Zeit hingewiesen, die man in eine Arbeit investiert.
Ja, ich habe festgestellt, dass durch die Zeitersparnis Erlebnis und sinnliche Erfahrung verloren geht.

Ihr Ansatz wird heute durch zahlreiche Ihrer ehemaligen Studierenden praktiziert und weitergegeben – nicht nur in der Schweiz [2] sondern auch in auffallend vielen Universitäten und Gestaltungsschulen in den USA. Wie kamen die engen Verbindungen zu den Vereinigten Staaten zustande?
Im März 1959 erhielt ich von Jean Koefoed, dem damaligen Verkaufsleiter des New Yorker Verlags Reinhold Publishing Corporation einen Brief, in dem er mir schrieb, dass er in der Zeitschrift *Graphis* mit grossem Interesse meinen Artikel zur formalen Erziehung des Gebrauchsgrafikers gelesen hatte. [5] Er meinte, dass noch nie eine Theorie zur Erziehung im Design-Bereich formuliert worden sei, obwohl in den USA ein so dringender Bedarf herrsche. Er schlug mir vor, diese Lücke zu schliessen und meinen Artikel zu einem Grundlagen bildenden Buch auszudehnen. So entstand die *Methodik der Form- und Bildgestaltung*. Dies zeigt, dass mein Konzept einer Grundausbildung nicht nur den Bedürfnissen Basels entsprach. Die gezeigten Beispiele der Ausbildung waren es auch, die mir bereits 1955 einen Lehrauftrag am Philadelphia College of Art und 1956 an der Yale University, New Haven, einbrachten. So ist mein Gedankengut durch ehemalige Studierende weitergetragen worden.

*1958 erschien erstmals die Zeitschrift *Neue Grafik* [6], doch kam es zu einer Art Entfremdung zwischen Ihnen und den Herausgebern. Was geschah damals?*
Das ursprüngliche Ziel, das ich mit Josef Müller-Brockmann verfolgte, war eine Zeitschrift, die qualitätvolle Arbeiten in der aktuellen angewandten Kunst behandeln sollte. Die Auffassungen der Beteiligten bewegte sich jedoch in die Richtung eines stilistischen Bekenntnisses, das mir zu eng gefasst schien. Mich interessierte das breite schöpferische Potential eines Entwurfs.

Es wird kolportiert, dass Sie niemals die Helvetica angewendet haben. Stimmt das?
Nein. Ich bin nicht der Typ, der sagt, ich habe diese oder jene Schrift lieber. Solche Dogmen haben mich nie interessiert. Mir war der Zeilenlauf oder die Graubildung viel wichtiger. Ich habe die Antiqua dann nicht angewendet, wenn sie in der Reduktion ihre Qualität verlor. Die Schönheit einer Serife ist nicht mehr sichtbar mit sieben oder acht Punkten. Mir ist eine serifenlose Schrift lieber, weil sie noch mit sechs Punkten lesbar ist und in ihrer Formentwicklung wahrnehmbar ist. Abgesehen davon sind Antiqua-Schriften vorbildlich.

Die Auseinandersetzung mit der Semiotik hat Ihre praktische und pädagogische Tätigkeit geprägt. Von wo kamen die entscheidenden Impulse?
Schon in meiner Jugendzeit stand mir der deutsche Frühromantiker Caspar David Friedrich sehr nahe, den ich aus der Sammlung Oskar Reinhart in Winterthur kannte. Die Symbolik seiner Bilder beinhaltete etwas, was mir später die Semiotik näherbrachte. In gewissem Sinne steht die Bedeutung des Mannes, der am Kreidefelsen steht schon nahe bei der Übersetzung in ein surreales Moment. [7] Schon sehr früh habe ich mich auch mit René Magritte beschäftigt. Max Ernst, Man Ray, Hans Arp... das war meine Welt.

Angeblich waren Sie einmal passionierter Leser von Thoreau. [8] Gab es noch andere Autoren oder Personen, die Ihr Denken prägten oder in denen Sie sich wiedererkannt haben?
Neben den Surrealisten war natürlich Kafka interessant für mich. Auch Max Frisch, mit dem ich in Aspen

war. Mit Mitscherlich[9] habe ich ein freundschaftliches Verhältnis gehabt. Er hat mich sehr beeindruckt.

Einer Ihrer Schüler erinnert sich, dass Sie den Unterricht unterbrochen haben und zwei Stunden lang Kafka vorgelesen haben.
Ja, das ist möglich. Mir war auch Musik immer sehr wichtig. Die Quartette von Hayden waren in Bezug auf Design sehr interessant. Was da an Wiederholung, an Variation, an Form und Geist vor sich geht, das war didaktisch unglaublich wertvoll! Und das habe ich auch versucht zu erklären.

Es fällt auf, dass Ihre Schüler für bestimmte Auftraggeber wie den Kinderverkehrsgarten, die Verkehrspolizei oder das Gewerbemuseum Basel regelmässig Plakate realisieren konnten. Haben Sie diese Aufträge ermöglicht?
Nein, das war eine Zusammenarbeit zwischen Staat und Schule. Von Grünigen war im Grossen Rat [dem Stadtparlament von Basel]. Dort kam jemand auf die Idee, Plakate durch die Schüler entwerfen zu lassen.

Was für einen Stellenwert hat dies für den Unterricht bekommen?
Für mich, der ständig Grundlagen vermittelte, war es interessant, diese einmal so breit wie möglich in die Praxis hineinzutragen. Diese Plakate haben ja alle einen didaktischen Kern. Sie sind aus den Übungen heraus entstanden, das war das Wunderbare. Und weil es zudem billig war, hat niemand dreingeredet. Diese Projekte waren als Wettbewerb angelegt, an dem meistens die ganze Klasse mitgemacht hat. Abgesehen davon war der Unterricht absolut individuell.
Nur selten haben mehrere Schüler an der gleichen Aufgabe gearbeitet. Und das war gegenseitig sehr inspirierend. Mein Anliegen war, die Persönlichkeit des einzelnen Schülers zu beachten, wenn ich eine Aufgabe stellte. Wenn ich sah, dass da jemand ist, der die Geometrie schätzt, dann habe ich

dort Übungen versucht zu entwickeln. Oder wenn ich sah: das ist ein Zeichner, dann habe ich versucht, mit ihm das zu entwickeln. Wenn jemand mit

Farben begabt war, habe ich sofort die Farbe in den Vordergrund gestellt.

Jeder hat also seine individuelle Förderaufgabe bekommen?
Ja. Das war für mich ein unheimlich anstrengender Prozess. Aber das war mein Weg.

Sie haben wiederholt betont, dass Sie Ihr eigenes Werk und Ihren Unterricht als gleichwertig auffassen. Erfüllten Ihre Plakate also auch einen didaktischen Zweck?
Ja, selbstverständlich.

Sind Ihre Plakate im Unterricht diskutiert worden?
Selbstverständlich. Die Schwarzweissplakate mit ihrer Zeichenhaftigkeit sind stark aus der Farbigkeit der Plakatwerbung herausgetreten. Natürlich hat das die Schüler animiert. Zu sehen, was man mit Nichts machen kann...

Wie hat der Offsetdruck Ihre Arbeit verändert?
Das war eine Erweiterung. Ich habe den Weggang vom Linolschnitt oder der Lithografie nicht als Einschränkung empfunden, sondern ich habe die modernen Möglichkeiten genutzt. Ich konnte durch den Offsetdruck erstmals die Fotografie mit den Zeichen verbinden. Die Plakate für das Stadttheater sind so möglich geworden. Die ganze Arbeit mit der Semiotik ist weitgehend durch den Offset denkbar geworden. Aber wichtig war, dass man für diese Drucktechnik ein grosses Vorstellungsvermögen entwickelte. Man muss gewisse Sachen schon im Kopf skizzieren.

Der Einbezug der Fotografie in die Grafik ist offensichtlich eng mit Ihrem damaligen Studenten Max Mathys verbunden. Wie muss man sich die Zusammenarbeit vorstellen?

Max Mathys begriff Wesen und Bedeutung der Fotografie. Es entstand eine enge Zusammenarbeit
im Lehramt und in der praktischen Tätigkeit. Mathys
erkannte das Zeichenhafte in der Fotografie.

Ihre Plakate sind, bis auf ganz wenige Ausnahmen,
für nicht-kommerzielle Auftraggeber gemacht worden.
Warum?
In der kommerziellen Werbung war damals eine
auf die Bedürfnisse des Marktes abgestimmte Plakatgestaltung üblich. Mir war es aber wichtig, eine
neue Formensprache zu entwickeln. Darüber hinaus
sollten meine Plakate auch eine didaktische
Wirkung haben. Die Industrie war daran nur bedingt
interessiert. Allerdings war die Firma Geigy eine
vorbildliche Ausnahme davon.[10]

Es fällt auf, dass Sie sehr behutsam mit Farbe umgingen.
War auch dies als eine Art Kommentar mit didaktischem
Hintergrund zu verstehen?
Ursprünglich waren die Plakate für die Kunsthalle
Basel nicht aus ästhetischen, sondern aus Kosten-
gründen schwarz und weiss. Aber es hat sich
ergeben, dass diese Einfachheit auch einen didaktischen Sinn bekam. Die Farbigkeit der Plakatwände
war so ungeordnet, dass jede sensible Farbsitua-
tion zerstört wurde. Das hat mich dazu bewogen, im
Plakat eher von der Farbe abzusehen. Es war mir
zu schade, ein farbiges Statement zu machen, weil
es in dieser Umgebung nicht durchkommt.

Welche Verantwortung trägt man, wenn man eine
Information visuell umsetzt?
In der heutigen Medienlandschaft wird alles sofort
tausendfach verbreitet. Das erhöht die
Verantwortung des Gestalters enorm. Deshalb sollte
an den Schulen eine entsprechende Haltung
vermittelt werden, eine mediale Ethik, die eine
umfassende Sicht ermöglicht.

[1] Lehrer an der Kunstgewerbeschule Zürich:
Heinrich Müller (1903–1978) unterrichtete 1930–1969
Zeichnen.
Walter Roshardt (1897–1966) unterrichtete 1926–1963
Zeichnen.
Carl Fischer (1888–1987) unterrichtete 1914–1954
Modellieren.
Alfred Willimann (1900–1957) unterrichtete 1929–1957
Schrift und Zeichnen.
Ernst Keller (1891–1968) unterrichtete 1918–1956 Grafik.
Ernst Gubler (1895–1958) unterrichtete 1932–1958
Zeichnen.
[2] Donald Brun (1909–1999) unterrichtete 1945–1974
Grafik an der Allgemeinen Gewerbeschule Basel (AGS).
[3] Emil Ruder (1914–1970), ab 1942 Fachlehrer für
Typografie, 1965–1970 Direktor der AGS Basel.
[4] Berchtold von Grünigen (*1899), 1943–1964 Direktor
der AGS Basel.
[5] Armin Hofmann, «Ein Beitrag zur formalen Erziehung
des Gebrauchsgrafikers/A Contribution to the Education
of the Commercial Artist», in: Graphis, Nr. 80, Zürich,
November/Dezember 1958.
[6] Neue Grafik erscheint 1958 bis 1965. Hg. Richard Paul
Lohse, Josef Müller-Brockmann, Hans Neuburg, Carlo
Vivarelli.
[7] Capar David Friedrich, Kreidefelsen auf Rügen,
ca. 1818, Museum Oskar Reinhart, Winterthur.
[8] Henry David Thoreau (1817–1862), amerikanischer
Schriftsteller und Sozialkritiker.
[9] Alexander Mitscherlich (1908–1982), Psychoanalytiker
und Sozialpsychologe.
[10] In der J. R. Geigy AG, einem Unternehmen der
chemischen Industrie Basels, waren seit Anfang der
1950er Jahre mehrere ehemalige Schüler Hofmanns
beschäftigt, die ihre Erfahrungen des Unterrichts
in die Praxis umsetzten und ein bemerkenswert
progressives Design prägen konnten.

INSERT

Auswahl von Plakaten von
Grafikerinnen und Grafikern, die
zwischen 1946 und 1986 bei
Armin Hofmann an der Allgemeinen Gewerbeschule Basel (AGS)
studierten.

A selection of posters by graphic
designers who studied under
Armin Hofmann at the Allgemeine
Gewerbeschule in Basel (AGS)
between 1946 and 1986.

1 Heinz Schenker
1959

2 Werner John
1959

3 Heinz Kroehl
1962

4 Ruth Pfalzberger
1969

5 Hermann Bausch
1970

6 Moritz Zwimpfer
1958

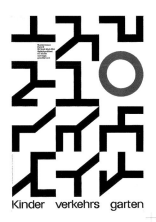

Georges Méliès
Beginn der Filmkunst
Gewerbemuseum Basel
23. Nov. bis
22. Dez. 1963

immer   frisch   erfrischt immer

26.Gesellschaftsausstellung
der schweizerischen
Malerinnen
Bildhauerinnen und
Kunstgewerblerinnen
7.Sept.-
13.Okt.

Kunsthalle
und
Gewerbe-
museum
Basel

messer gabel löffel

6. Eidg.
Harmonika
Musikfest
25.   27. Juni
1971

Riehen

Garantiert
frisch!
Dänische
Eier!

sorgenlos
in der
SBB

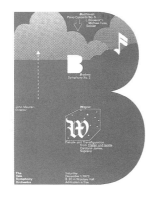

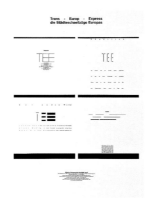

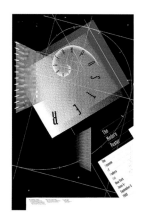

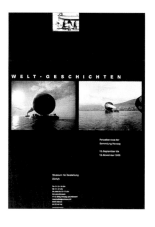

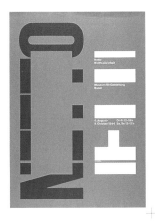

EXCERPTS FROM AN INTERVIEW
WITH ARMIN HOFMANN

Lucerne, February 2003
Felix Studinka

You signed on for courses at the Kunstgewerbeschule in Zurich in 1937 and 1938. What did you expect from the school?
I wanted to acquire a deeper understanding of my drawing talents at the school.

Who were your mentors, and what did you learn from them?
I was impressed by all the staff: Heinrich Müller, Walter Roshard, the sculptor Fischer, later Alfred Willimann and Ernst Keller as well, but Ernst Gubler most of all.[1] It wasn't the style of their work that impressed me, but their seriousness and their attitude; this gave their work its underlying meaning.

To what extent were you aware of constructive concepts in commercial graphics at that time?
I wasn't aware of them at all. I didn't know anything then about the whole group around Max Bill, Richard Paul Lohse, Camille Graeser etc.

In 1937, at the age of 27 and coming from Zurich, you got your first steady job at the Allgemeine Gewerbeschule in Basel. Donald Brun,[2] who was utterly committed to Basel's illustrative tradition and to craft, had just started teaching there. Were you supposed to be a young outsider representing "Modernism"?
No, it was just coincidence. I was working for Fritz Bühler in Basel as a lithographer at the time. I happened to meet Ruder[3] one the train to Zurich on day. I was reading a little book about van Gogh, and so we got talking. He said they'd be looking for a teacher, and that I should get in touch with the school. Later the director of the school, von Grünigen,[4] rang me up because he wanted to make me Brun's assistant. Von Grünigen had taught me while I was doing my lithography apprenticeship in Zurich. I wasn't brought in as an innovator, it wasn't like that at all. I grew into things very slowly.

Was this how you found out that you had a talent for teaching?
I sensed that the pupils needed to go back to basics. When I took over a course with Brun later, I started trying to convey basic principles, and von Grünigen realized that this could lead to an ideal dialogue in terms of creative exploration. Brun was an admirable person, and he never put any obstacles in my way. I must have been an educator without knowing. I didn't have any experience.

At what point did you become aware that you had developed your own method?
That came very slowly. I tried to convey simplicity in all its complexity very comprehensibly and practically by teaching an intensive study of elementary geometrical elements like the point or the line, for example, to enable pupils to make more profound formal development links. Making something simple had made it complex. Reduction to simplicity required knowledge and feeling. It was not a method, it was an approach. The teaching concept gradually grew out of this, and the pupils found it very interesting.

What made your teaching so much in demand internationally?
Precisely that: people could see that this was a combination of basic training and application, and that's what made the teaching appealing.

Terms like cleanness, simplicity and concentration were very important in your education. Were ideals like that also involved in promoting a mental approach?
Yes, there above all. The process produces a mental attitude.

Your teaching was much more comprehensive than is usually expected from this training.
Of course. What I wanted to convey was not in the first place advertising, but a study of the world of images.

You linked the claim to be Modern with an ethical claim. This is reminiscent of the spirit of Ulm. Were there connections with the Hochschule für Gestaltung in Ulm?
No, there weren't any connections. Ulm scarcely took any notice of the Basel course, as it didn't have university status. Basel was a vocational school that followed its own ethic.

You have witnessed an incredible development from lithography to the computer. How did this development affect your teaching? How did you prepare your students for developments of this kind?
In exactly the opposite way from the one you might think of. It became increasingly clear to me that basics are getting more important. The more technical the world is, the more the system breaks up, the more important it becomes to convey basics. So I tried to develop model exercises as processes that were complete in themselves: from the idea via the sketch to the design to realization. So that you can see the process. I realized that it is fatal if there are photocopiers standing around in schools where any old nonsense can be copied immediately and varied a hundred times, and at the end there are thousands of attempts around and no one knows what has

actually happened. I'd rather someone went over his own work a hundred times with a pencil and gained some sort of insight. The line means a great deal to me in drawing terms, and that's precisely what I paid most attention to: an element creeps in here almost unnoticed, and it's something that has acquired exemplary significance in human history, in nature, in architecture, painting, typography or in everyday objects.

You have always pointed out the importance of the time invested in work.
Yes, I realized that you lose experience and sensuality by saving time.

Your approach is practised and passed on today by countless of your former students – not just in Switzerland but in a striking number of universities and design schools in the USA. How did your close links with the United States come about?
In March 1959, Jan Koefoed, who was then sales director of the New York Reinhold Publishing Corporation, wrote me a letter in which he said that he had been very interested to read my article about the formal education of commercial artists in the magazine *Graphis*.[5] He felt that there had never been a theory of design education, even though it was urgently needed in the USA. He suggested I might like to fill this gap by expanding my article to form the basis of an educational book. This is how the *Graphic Design Manual* came into being. This shows that my concept of basic training did not just meet the needs of Basel. The teaching examples I gave also led to a teaching post at the Philadelphia College of Art as early as 1955, and at Yale University, New Haven in 1956. So my ideas were passed on by former students.

The magazine *Neue Grafik*[6] appeared for the first time in 1958, but there was a sort of falling-out between you and the editors. What happened at the time?
The original aim that I pursued with Josef Müller-Brockmann was a magazine that would deal with high-quality work in contemporary applied art. But the views of those involved tended towards a stylistic commitment that seemed too tightly drawn to me. I was interested in the broad creative potential of a design.

Rumour has it that you have never used Helvetica. Is that true?
No. I'm not the sort of person who says I prefer this or that typeface. I have never been interested in dogmas like that. I was much more interested in the line arrangement and the grey balance. I didn't use roman type when it lost quality in reduction. You can't see the beauty of a seven- or eight-point serif.

I go for a sans-serif type because you can still read it in a six-point version and be aware of its formal development. Apart from that, roman typefaces are exemplary.

Your study of semiotics greatly affected your practical and pedagogic activities. Where did the key thrust come from?
I was very sympathetic to the early German Romantic painter Caspar David Friedrich, whose work I knew from the Oskar Reinhart Collection in Winterthur. The symbolism of his pictures involved something that brought me very close to semiotics later. In a certain sense the significance of the man standing by the chalk cliff[7] comes very close to tilting over into the surreal. I looked at René Magritte at a very early stage as well. Max Ernst, Man Ray, Hans Arp... that was my world.

Apparently you were a passionate reader of Thoreau.[8] Were there other authors or people who shaped your thinking or who you recognized yourself in?
Of course I was very interested in Kafka as well as the Surrealists. Max Frisch as well, I was in Aspen with him. I was on friendly terms with Mitscherlich.[9] He impressed me a great deal.

One of your pupils remembers that you stopped teaching once and read Kafka out loud for two hours.
Yes, that is possible. Music was always very important to me as well. Haydn's quartets were very interesting in relation to design. What is happening there in the form of repetition, variation, form and spirit was incredibly valuable didactically! And I tried to explain it as well.

It's noticeable that your pupils had the opportunity to design posters for the "Kinderverkehrsgarten", the transport police and the Gewerbemuseum in Basel. Did you bring these commission about?
No, the school and the state worked together on that. Von Grünigen was in the Grosser Rat [Basel's city

parliament]. Someone there had the idea of letting the students design the posters.

What was the value of this in terms of teaching?
I was constantly passing on basic principles, and so it was interesting to put this into practice on as broad a basis as possible. All these posters have a didactic core. The wonderful thing was that they grew out of the exercises. And because it was cheap as well, no one interfered. These projects were organized as competitions, and the whole class was involved most of the time. Apart from that the teaching was absolutely individual.
It was rare for several students to work on the same project at once. And the inspiration worked both ways. I was interested in taking an individual pupil's personality into account when I set a piece of work. When I spotted someone who really appreciated geometry I tried to develop exercises around that. Or when I thought: we've got a draughtsman here, I tried to develop that with him. If someone had a gift for handling colour, I immediately made the colour the main thing.

So everyone was brought on individually by the work they were set?
Yes. It was an incredibly demanding process for me. But that was how I worked.

You have repeatedly stressed that you see your own work and your teaching as equally valuable. So did your posters have a didactic purpose?
Yes, of course.

Were your posters discussed in lessons?
Of course. The black-and-white posters with their sign quality stood out against colour poster advertising. Of course that stimulates your pupils. Seeing what can be done with nothing…

How did offset printing change your work?
It took things further. I did not see the departure from linocuts or lithography as a restriction, I used the opportunities offered by modern developments. Offset printing let me combine photography with signs for the first time. This is what made the posters for the Stadttheater possible. All the work using semiotics was largely conceivable because of offset. But an important factor was that a great deal of imagination was needed for this printing technique. You have to sketch out certain things in advance in your mind.

Including photography in graphics is obviously closely linked with Max Mathys, who was your student at the time. How should we picture you working together?
Max Mathys understood the nature and significance of photography. It led to close co-operation in teaching and in terms of practical activity. Mathys recognized the sign quality of photography.

With a very few exceptions, your posters were designed for non-commercial clients. Why?
At that time, poster design matched to market needs was customary for commercial advertising. But I was concerned with developing a new formal language. And my posters were supposed to make a didactic impact as well. The industry was only interested in that to a limited extent. Though Geigy was an exemplary exception here.[10]

It's noticeable that you handled colour very cautiously. Was this to be seen as a kind of comment with a didactic background?
Originally the Kunsthalle Basel posters were black and white for reasons of cost rather than aesthetics. But it turned out that this simplicity made didactic sense as well. The colours on the advertisement hoardings were so chaotic that any sensitive colour scheme was destroyed. That is why I decided I'd prefer to do without colour in my posters. It seemed a shame to make a colour statement because it didn't come over in this context.

What responsibilities come with conveying information visually?

In today's media landscape everything is always passed on a thousand times over. This increases the designer's responsibility enormously. For this reason the schools should pass on an appropriate approach, a media ethic that makes a comprehensive view possible.

[1] Teachers at the Kunstgewerbeschule in Zürich:
Heinrich Müller 1903–1978 taught drawing 1930–1969.
Walter Roshardt 1897–1966 taught drawing 1926–1963.
Carl Fischer 1888–1987 taught modelling 1914–1954.
Alfred Willimann 1900–1957 taught typography and drawing 1929–1957.
Ernst Keller 1891–1968 taught graphics 1918–1956.
Ernst Gubler 1895–1958 taught drawing 1932–1958.
[2] Donald Brun 1909–1999, taught graphics at the Allgemeine Gewerbeschule Basel (AGS) 1945–1974.
[3] Emil Ruder 1914–1970, typography teacher from 1942, 1965–1970 director of the AGS Basel.
[4] Berchtold von Grünigen 1899–1976, 1943–1964 director of the AGS Basel.
[5] Armin Hofmann, "Ein Beitrag zur formalen Erziehung des Gebrauchsgrafikers / A Contribution to the Education of the Commercial Artist", in: *Graphis,* no. 80, Zurich, November / December 1958.
[6] *Neue Grafik* appeared from 1958 to 1965. Ed. Richard Paul Lohse, Josef Müller-Brockmann, Hans Neuburg, Carlo Vivarelli.
[7] Capar David Friedrich, Kreidefelsen auf Rügen (Chalk Cliffs on Rügen), c.1818, Museum Oskar Reinhart, Winterthur.
[8] Henry David Thoreau 1817–1862. American writer and social critic.
[9] Alexander Mitscherlich 1908–1982. Psychoanalyst and social psychologist.
[10] Many of Hofmann's former pupils worked for J. R. Geigy AG, a Basel chemical company, from the early 1950s, putting what they had been taught into practice and thus able to create remarkably progressive design.

Kunsthalle
Basel
Jacques Lipchitz
9. Aug.-
7. Sept.

48 **Jacques Lipchitz**
1958

Kunsterziehung in **Usa**
Gewerbemuseum Basel
1. Sept.-7.Okt. Eintritt frei
Täglich geöffnet: 10-12 und 14-17 Uhr, Mittwoch auch 20-22 Uhr

Litho: A. Hofmann / Druck: Wassermann AG.

49 Kunsterziehung in USA
Art Education in the USA
1962

17. Juni-16. Juli
und 5.-20. August
10-12, 14-17 Uhr
Mittwoch auch
20-22 Uhr
Täglich geöffnet
Eintritt frei

Plakate aus der
Sammlung
des
Gewerbe
museums
Basel

50 Plakat aus der Sammlung des Gewerbemuseums Basel
Posters from the Gewerbemuseum Basel's Collection
1961

Entwurf: A.Hofmann / Druck: Wassermann A.G.

Schweiz
kleines Land
grosse
Landschaft

51 Schweiz / kleines Land grosse Landschaft
Switzerland / Small Country Big Landscape
ca. 1965

Stadt
Theater
Basel

52 **Stadttheater Basel**
1962

Stadttheater Basel
Beginn der Spielzeit 1961/62
am 14. September 1961

Eröffnungspremieren:
Pelléas und Melisande
Musikdrama von Débussy
Richard II
Trauerspiel von Shakespeare
Die Entführung aus dem Serail
Oper von Mozart
Zurück zur Natur
Komödie von Barrie

Profitieren auch Sie
von den großen Vorteilen
des Abonnements:
Bedeutende Preisermäßigung
Fester Platz für alle
Vorstellungen
Zahlung des Abonnements-
preises in zwei Raten

Wir legen folgende
Abonnements auf:

Premieren-Abonnement für
25 Vorstellungen

Wochentag-Abonnement
Montag, Mittwoch oder Freitag
für 25 Vorstellungen

Schauspiel-Abonnement für
10 Schauspiel-
Aufführungen mit 50 Prozent
Preisermäßigung

**Stadt
theater
Basel**

53 **Stadttheater Basel 1961/62**
1961

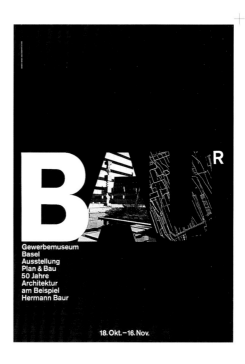

54 The Museum of Modern Art New York /
Armin Hofmann / Posters
1981

55 Staatlicher Kunstkredit Basel-Stadt 1985/86
Basel-Stadt State Art Credit 1985/86
1985

56 Baur
1975

57 J. Brahms / Ein Deutsches Requiem
1986

1966 \ 67
Stadttheater
Basel

Entwurf: A. Hofmann / Druck: Wassermann A.G.

58 Stadttheater Basel 1966/67
1966

Während der Saison 1967/68 finden Sie an dieser Stelle den Spielplan.

Der Saisonprospekt ist erschienen; er orientiert Sie über den Spielplan, das Ensemble und die günstigen Abonnements.

Stadt
theater
Basel

59 **Stadttheater Basel 1967/68**
1967

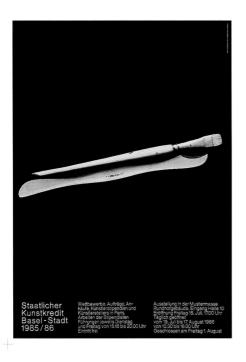

60 [Brot] für Brüder
[Bread] for Brothers
1970

61 Staatlicher Kunstkredit Basel-Stadt 1985/86
Basel-Stadt State Art Credit 1985/86
1986

62 Basel/kostbares Erbe/schöpferische Gegenwart
Basel/Precious Heritage/Creative Present
1968

63 Stadttheater Basel 1964/65
1964

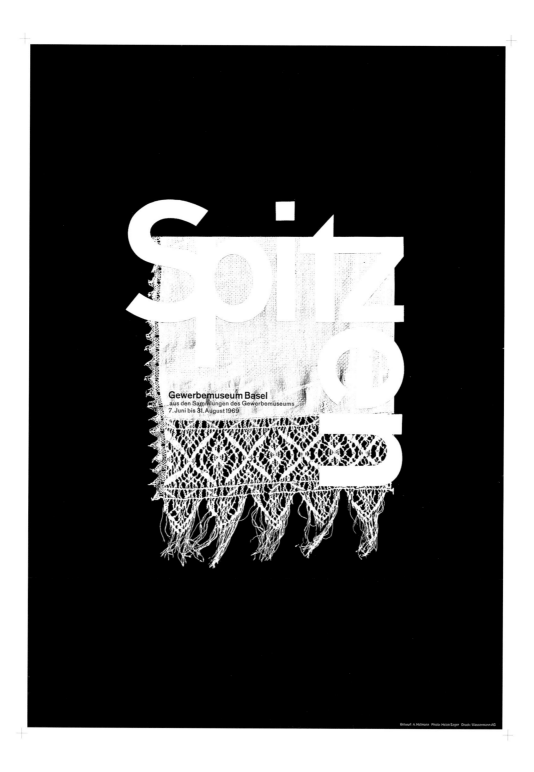

64 **Spitzen – Lace**
1969

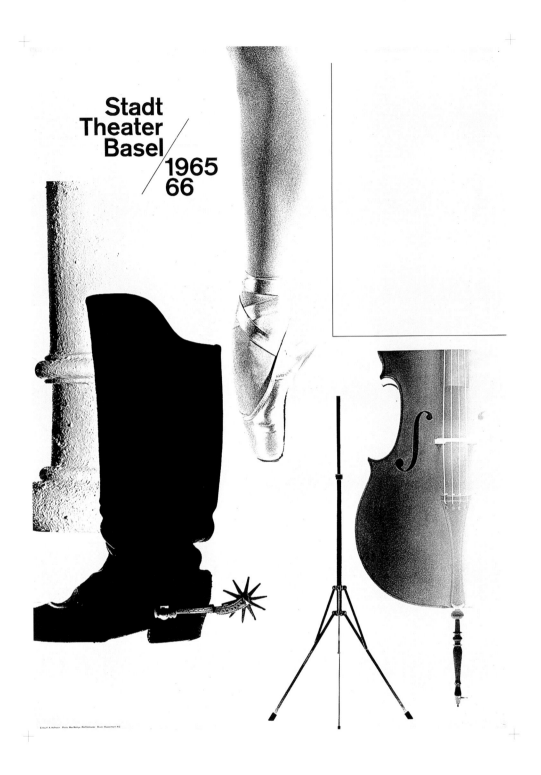

Stadt
Theater
Basel / 1965
66

65 **Stadttheater Basel 1965/66**
1965

66 **Giselle**
1959

Basler Freilichtspiele
beim Letziturm im St. Albantal
I5.-3I. VIII 1963

Wilhelm Tell

67 **Wilhelm Tell**
1963

Biografie

Armin Hofmann wird am 29. Juni 1920 in Winterthur geboren. 1937–38 besucht er den künstlerischen Vorkurs an der Kunstgewerbeschule Zürich, absolviert anschliessend eine Zeichner-Lithografenlehre in Winterthur und besucht weiterbildende Kurse in Zürich. Ab 1943 ist er in verschiedenen Ateliers als Lithograf und Entwerfer tätig, u. a. bei der Frobenius AG und im Atelier Fritz Bühler, beide in Basel.

1947 wird er an der Allgemeinen Gewerbeschule Basel (AGS, später Schule für Gestaltung) eingestellt und unterrichtet in der Fachklasse für Grafik neben Donald Brun. Hier entwickelt er ein Unterrichtsverfahren für künstlerische und gestalterische Berufe, das breite Anerkennung gewinnt und 1955 zu einer Gastprofessur am Philadelphia College of Art führt. Es folgt eine Berufung an die Yale University, wo er regelmässig Arbeitsseminarien für Grafik durchführt. 1957 wird Hofmann in den Lehrkörper der Kunstgewerblichen Abteilung der AGS gewählt und 1967 zum Leiter der Fachklasse für Gebrauchsgrafik ernannt. Die liberale Praxis der Schulleitung ermöglicht ihm weiterhin, im Ausland zu lehren. So ist er 1965 für sechs Monate Berater und Dozent am National Institute of Design in Ahmedabad, Indien. Eine besonders enge Verbindung stellt sich zur Yale University ein, wo er bis 1991 regelmässig unterrichtet. 1965 legt er sein Buch «Methodik der Form- und Bildgestaltung» (Niggli Verlag, Teufen) vor, das sich als Standardwerk etabliert. Entsprechend der von ihm geforderten grundlegenden Ausbildung für Grafiker, gründet Hofmann 1968 mit Emil Ruder den Weiterbildungskurs für visuelle Gestaltung an der AGS, der eine starke internationale Ausstrahlung entwickelt. Als Mitglied der Direktorenkonferenz der Schweizerischen Kunstgewerbeschulen ist er ab 1971 an der Koordinierung der nationalen Ausbildungsprogramme beteiligt. Hofmann ist Initiant des Summer Program in Graphic Design in Brissago, einer Intensiv-Weiterbildung in idyllischer Umgebung, 1974–81 in Verbindung mit der Kent State University, dann 1982–96 mit der Yale University.

Nach vierzig Jahren Lehrtätigkeit in Basel tritt Hofmann 1986 in den Ruhestand. Sein Werk beinhaltet neben Plakaten auch Signete, Akzidenzen, Bücher, Ausstellungen, Bühnenbilder, Farbkonzepte, Orientierungssysteme sowie Kunst-am-Bau-Projekte.
Armin Hofmann erhält zahlreiche Ehrungen für sein Werk: 1987 wird er Ehrendoktor der Philadelphia University of the Arts, 1988 Ehrenmitglied der Royal Society of Arts, London und 1997 wird ihm der Kulturpreis der Stadt Basel verliehen.

Biography

Armin Hofmann was born on 29 June 1920 in Winterthur. In 1937–38 he attended the art foundation course at the Kunstgewerbeschule in Zurich, then did a draughtsmanship and lithography apprenticeship in Winterthur and followed further education course in Zurich. He worked in various studios as a lithographer and designer from 1943, including Frobenius AG and Atelier Fritz Bühler, both in Basel.

He was employed by the Allgemeine Gewerbeschule in Basel (AGS, later Schule für Gestaltung) and taught the advanced graphics course with Donald Brun. Here he developed a widely appreciated teaching method for the art and design professions, and this led to a visiting professorship at the Philadelphia College of Art in 1955. Then came an appointment at Yale University, where he regularly conducted working seminars in graphic art. Hofmann became a permanent member of the AGS art department in 1957, and director of the advanced graphics course in 1967. The school's liberal approach meant that he could carry on teaching abroad. Thus he became adviser and lecturer at the National Institute of Design in Ahmedabad, India, in 1956; he developed particularly close links with Yale University, and taught there regularly until 1991. He published his book "Methodik der Form- und Bildgestalung" (Graphic Design Manual; Niggli Verlag, Teufen) in 1965, which established itself as a standard work. In 1968, Hofmann and Emil Ruder set up the visual design further education course at the AGS, to provide the basic training for graphic artists that he had always promoted, and this soon acquired a strong international reputation. As a member of the Directors' Conference of Swiss Applied Art Schools he was involved in co-ordinating the national training programme from 1971. Hofmann initiated the Summer Program in Graphic Design in Brissago, an intensive further education course in idyllic surroundings, in association with Kent State University in 1974–81, then with Yale University in 1982–96.

Hofmann retired in 1986, after forty years of teaching in Basel. As well as posters, his work includes logos, jobbing printing, books, exhibitions, stage sets, colour concepts, signing systems and art-in-building projects.
Armin Hofmann has received numerous honours for his work: an honorary doctorate at the Philadelphia University of the Arts in 1987, honorary membership of the Royal Society of Arts London in 1988, and he was awarded the City of Basel Culture Prize in 1997.

Katalog

Die abgebildeten Plakate stammen bis auf zwei Ausnahmen aus der Plakatsammlung des Museums
für Gestaltung Zürich. Das Plakat Nr. 42 wurde uns
freundlicherweise aus einer privaten Sammlung
zur Verfügung gestellt. Nr. 55 existiert nicht mehr.

Die Daten des Katalogs folgen den Rubriken Gestaltung, Plakattext, Erscheinungsjahr, Drucktechnik und
Format. Dabei gelten folgende Regelungen:

Gestaltung: Es werden der vollständige Name, die
Lebensdaten und der heutige Wirkungsort angegeben.

Plakattext: Die beste Textwiedergabe bildet die
Abbildung des Plakates selbst. Darum wird hier eine
vereinfachte Form wiedergegeben, welche nur die
aussagekräftigsten Textbestandteile berücksichtigt.
Allfällige Umstellungen dienen der Verständlichkeit.
Das Zeichen / trennt inhaltliche Texteinheiten.

Drucktechnik: Die englische Übersetzung der Drucktechnik erschliesst sich meist aus dem deutschen
Begriff wie Lithografie oder Offset.

Format: Die Angaben werden in der Abfolge
Höhe × Breite und in cm gemacht. Weil die Plakate
nicht immer exakt rechtwinklig geschnitten sind,
werden die Abmessungen auf halbe cm aufgerundet.

Die Plakatgeschichte ist ein junges Forschungsgebiet –
verlässliche Informationen sind rar. Jeder Hinweis und
jede Ergänzung sind willkommen:
plakat.sammlung@museum-gestaltung.ch.

**Armin Hofmann hat seine Plakate in sieben Gruppen
verschiedener gestalterischer Probleme gefasst.
In der Eingangssequenz dieses Buches (1–7) ist aus
jeder Kategorie ein Beispiel abbgebildet:**

1 Typografische Lösungen. Zeilen- und Gruppenbildung
2 Form und Ausdruck des Einzelbuchstabens
3 Konfrontationen Kombinationen Abwandlungen
4 Freie Schriftformen und Schriftbilder
5 Vereinfachung und Abstraktion gegenständlicher
Motive
6 Fotografische Zeichen mit reduzierter typografischer
Information
7 Wort-Bild-Beziehungen im Sinne semiotischer
Verhältnisse

Catalogue

With two exceptions, the posters illustrated come from
the Museum für Gestaltung Zürich's Poster Collection.
Poster no. 42 was kindly loaned by a private collector.
No. 55 does not exist anymore.

The data in the catalogue are under the headings
design, poster text, year of appearance, country of first
appearance, printing technique, format. The following
rules have been applied:

Design: the full name and dates of birth and the present
base for activities are given.

Poster text: the poster itself provides the best version
of the text. Thus a simplified form is used here, giving
only the most meaningful elements of the text. Any
rearrangements that have been made are for purposes
of intelligibility. The sign / separates textual units
by content.

Printing technique: the English translation of the
printing technique is usually suggested by the German
concept, as in Lithografie or Offset. Buchdruck means
letterpress, Linolschnitt means lino cut.

Format: the details are given in the sequence
height × width and in cm. Because the posters are
often not cut exactly at right angles, the dimensions
are rounded off to half cm.

The history of posters is a recent field of research –
reliable information is rare. Any references or additional
material are welcome:
plakat.sammlung@museum-gestaltung.ch

**Armin Hofmann has arranged his posters in seven
groups addressing various design problems.
One example from each category is illustrated in
the opening sequence of this book (1–7):**

1 Typographic solutions, forming lines and groups
2 Form and expression from an individual letter
3 Confrontations combinations variations
4 Free type forms and typefaces
5 Simplification and abstraction for figurative motifs
6 Photographic signes with reduced typographic
information
7 Word-image connections in semiotic relations

1 Henry Moore/Oskar
Schlemmer/Kunsthalle Basel
1955
Linolschnitt, Buchdruck 127 × 90

2 Robert Jacobsen/Serge
Poliakoff/Kunsthalle Basel
1958
Linolschnitt, Buchdruck 127 × 90

3 Stadtthater Basel 63/64
Foto: Max Mathys
1963
Offset 128 × 90,5

4 Das Holz als Baustoff
Wood as a Building Material/
Gewerbemuseum Basel
1952
Linolschnitt, Buchdruck 127 × 90

5 Basler Theater 1968/9
Theatre in Basel 1968/9
1968
Offset 128 × 90

6 Graham Sutherland/
El Lissitzky/Kunsthalle Basel
1966
Linolschnitt, Buchdruck 127 × 90

7 Stadttheater Basel 1960/61
Foto: Paul Merkle
1960
Offset 127 × 90

8 Mark Rothko/Eduardo Chillida/
Kunsthalle Basel
1962
Lithografie, Buchdruck 127 × 90

9 René Auberjonois/Ernest
Bolens/Kunsthalle Basel
1961
Buchdruck 127 × 90

10 Hans Fischer/Ernst Georg
Rüegg/Kunsthalle Basel
1959
Linolschnitt, Buchdruck 127 × 90

11 Paul Burckhardt/Emil Schill/
Carlo König/Kunsthalle Basel
1961
Offset 127 × 90

12 Junge spanische Maler
Young Spanish Painters/
Kunsthalle Basel
1959
Linolschnitt, Buchdruck 127 × 90

13 Sammlung Cavellini
Cavellini Collection/
Kunsthalle Basel
1958
Linolschnitt, Buchdruck 127 × 90

14 Junge holländische Bildhauer
Young Dutch Sculptors/
Kunsthalle Basel
1960
Linolschnitt, Buchdruck 127 × 90

15 Maurice Estève/Berto
Lardera/Kunsthalle Basel
1961
Linolschnitt, Buchdruck 127 × 90

16 Basler Bach Chor
Basel Bach Choir
1980
Offset 128 × 90,5

17 David Smith/Horst Janssen/
Kunsthalle Basel
1966
Offset 127 × 90

18 Deutsche Künstler der
Gegenwart
Contemporary German Artists/
Kunsthalle Basel
1959
Linolschnitt, Buchdruck 127 × 90

19 Walter J. Moeschlin/
Kunsthalle Basel
1969
Offset 128 × 90,5

20 Willi Baumeister/Ernst
Wilhelm Nay/Kunsthalle Basel
1960
Linolschnitt, Buchdruck 127 × 90

21 Fernand Léger/Alexander
Calder/Kunsthalle Basel
1957
Linolschnitt, Buchdruck 127 × 90

22 Junge Berliner Künstler
Young Berlin Artists/Kunsthalle
Basel
1966
Offset 127 × 90

23 Ernst Morgenthaler/
Kunsthalle Basel
1962
Offset 127 × 90

24 Wilfredo Lam/Vic Gentils/
Kunsthalle Basel
1966
Offset 127 × 90

25 Phillip Martin/Ennio Morlotti/
Hans R. Schiess/Kunsthalle Basel
1967
Linolschnitt, Buchdruck 127 × 90

26 Franz Kline/Alfred Jensen/
Kunsthalle Basel
1964
Linolschnitt, Buchdruck 127 × 90

27 Die gute Form
Good Design/
SWB Mustermesse Basel
1954
Offset 128 × 90,5

28 R. Adams/7 junge englische
Maler
R. Adams/7 Young English
Painters/Kunsthalle Basel
1963
Offset 127 × 90

29 Aeschbacher/Bill/Müller/
Linck/4 Bildhauer
Aeschbacher/Bill/Müller/Linck/
4 Sculptors/Kunsthalle Basel
1959
Offset 127 × 90

30 Christoph Iselin/Walter
Schneider/Jacques Düblin/
Karl Moor/Kunsthalle Basel
1964
Lithografie 127 × 90

31 Karl Geiser/Kunsthalle Basel
1957
Linolschnitt, Buchdruck 127 × 90

32 Tempel und Teehaus in Japan
Temple and Teahouse in Japan/
Gewerbemuseum Basel
1955
Linolschnitt, Buchdruck 127 × 90

33 Kreis 48/Kunsthalle Basel
1950
Lithografie, Buchdruck 127 × 90

34 Walter Bodmer/Otto
Tschumi/Teruko Yokoi/
Kunsthalle Basel
1964
Offset 128 × 90,5

35 Heinrich Müller/Marguerite
Ammann/Walter J. Moeschlin/
Kunsthalle Basel
1957
Offset 127 × 90

36 Moderne Malerei seit 1945
aus der Sammlung Dotremont
Modern Painting since 1945
from the Dotremont Collection/
Kunsthalle Basel
1961
Linolschnitt, Buchdruck 127 × 90

37 Felix Vallotton und Kunst
des Ostens
Felix Vallotton and the Art of the
East/Kunsthalle Basel
1957
Offset 127 × 90

38 Die Schweiz zur Römerzeit
Switzerland in Roman Times /
Mustermesse Basel
1957
Lithografie 127 × 90

39 Münster-Scheiben-Entwürfe
und Glasbilder von Charles
Hindenlang im Gewerbemuseum
Basel
Minster Pane Designs and Stained
Glass by Charles Hindenlang
in the Gewerbemuseum Basel
1952
Linolschnitt, Buchdruck 127 × 90

40 Photographie in der Schweiz
Photography in Switzerland /
Gewerbemuseum Basel
1949
Linolschnitt, Buchdruck 127 × 90

41 Siedlungsbau in der Schweiz
1938–47
Housing Estate Construction in
Switzerland 1938–47 /
Gewerbemuseum Basel
1948
Linolschnitt, Buchdruck 127 × 90

42 Rheinau-Initiative Ja
Rheinau Yes Initiative
1954
Lithografie 128 × 90
Privatsammlung

43 Ohr + Auge /
Wir eröffnen am 16. September
Ear + Eye /
We open on September 16 /
Stadttheater Basel
1955
Offset 127 × 90

44 Theaterbau von der Antike
bis zur Moderne
Theatre construction in Antiquity
and Modernity /
Helmhaus Zürich
1955
Linolschnitt, Buchdruck 127 × 90

45 Basel und die Stadtstrassen
der Zukunft
Basel and the urban roads of the
future / Gewerbemuseum Basel
1961
Linolschnitt, Buchdruck 127 × 90

46 Herman Miller Collection /
Möbel unserer Zeit
Herman Miller Collection /
Furniture of our Times
1962
Offset 127 × 90

47 Alte und neue Formen in
Japan
Old and New Forms in Japan /
Gewerbemuseum Basel
1959
Linolschnitt, Buchdruck 127 × 90

48 Jacques Lipchitz /
Kunsthalle Basel
1958
Linolschnitt, Buchdruck 127 × 90

49 Kunsterziehung in USA
Art Education in the USA /
Gewerbemuseum Basel
1962
Offset 127 × 90

50 Plakat aus der Sammlung des
Gewerbemuseums Basel
Posters from the Gewerbemuseum
Basel's Collection
1961
Linolschnitt, Buchdruck 127 × 90

51 Schweiz / kleines Land
grosse Landschaft
Switzerland / small country big
landscape
Foto: anonym
ca. 1965
Offset 128 × 90

52 Stadttheater Basel
1962
Offset 128 × 90
Basler Plakatsammlung

53 Stadttheater Basel 1961/62
Foto: anonym
1961
Offset 128 × 90,5

54 The Museum of Modern Art
New York / Armin Hofmann /
Posters
Foto: Max Mathys
1981
Offset 91,5 × 61

55 Staatlicher Kunstkredit Basel-
Stadt 1985/86
Basel-Stadt State Art Credit
1985/86
1985
Layout / Entwurf ca. 42 × 30

56 Baur / Gewerbemuseum Basel
1975
Offset 127 × 90

57 J. Brahms / Ein Deutsches
Requiem / Basler Münster
Foto: anonym
1986
Offset 128 × 90,5

58 Stadttheater Basel 1966/67
Foto: Max Mathys
1966
Offset 127 × 90

59 Stadttheater Basel 1967/68
Foto: Max Mathys
1967
Offset 127 × 90

60 [Brot] für Brüder
[Bread] for Brothers
Foto: Max Mathys
1970
Offset 127 × 90

61 Staatlicher Kunstkredit
Basel-Stadt 1985/86
Basel-Stadt State Art Credit
1985/86
Foto: Max Mathys
1986
Offset 128 × 90,5

62 Basel / kostbares Erbe /
schöpferische Gegenwart
Basel / Precious Heritange /
Creative Present
Foto: Max Mathys
1968
Offset 127 × 90

63 Stadttheater Basel 1964/65
Foto: Max Mathys
1964
Offset 127 × 90

64 Spitzen
Lace / Gewerbemuseum Basel
Foto: Helen Sager
1969
Offset 128 × 90,5

65 Stadttheater Basel 1965/66
Foto: Max Mathys
1965
Offset 127 × 90

66 Giselle / Basler Freilichtspiele
Foto: Paul Merkle
1959
Offset 127 × 90

67 Wilhelm Tell / Basler Freilichtspiele
Foto: Max Mathys
1963
Offset 128 × 90,5

Auswahl von Plakaten von Grafikerinnen und Grafikern, die zwischen 1946 und 1986 bei Armin Hofmann an der Allgemeinen Gewerbeschule Basel (AGS) studierten.

A selection of posters by graphic designers who studied under Armin Hofmann at the Allgemeine Gewerbeschule in Basel (AGS) between 1946 and 1986

1 Heinz Schenker (*1940)
Cincinnati
AGS 1956–1960
Kinderverkehrsgarten
1959
CH Lithografie 128 × 90,5

2 Werner John (*1941)
AGS 1957–1961
Kinderverkehrsgarten
1959
CH Linolschnitt, Buchdruck
127 × 90

3 Heinz Kroehl (*1937)
Frankfurt am Main
AGS 1960–1964
Kinderverkehrsgarten
1962
CH Offset 128 × 90,5

4 Ruth Pfalzberger (*1949)
Basel
AGS 1964–1969
Kinderverkehrsgarten
1969
CH Offset 128 × 90

5 Hermann Bausch
verbleib unbekannt
Kinderverkehrsgarten
1970
CH Offset 127 × 90

6 Moritz Zwimpfer (*1940)
Basel
AGS 1958–1962
Kinderverkehrsgarten
1958
CH Linolschnitt, Buchdruck
128 × 90,5

7 Igildo Biesele (*1930)
Biel-Benken
AGS 1945–1949
Marionetten
Marionettes/
Gewerbemuseum Winterthur
1955
CH Linolschnitt, Buchdruck
128 × 90,5

8 Karl Gerstner (*1930)
Basel
AGS 1950/51
Bech Electronic Center
Gerstner + Kutter
1959
CH Offset 128 × 90,5

9 Andreas His (*1928)
Witterswil
AGS 1945–1950
Bild-Teppiche
Picture Carpets/
Gewerbemuseum Basel
1953
CH Linolschnitt, Buchdruck
127 × 90

10 Gérard Ifert (*1929)
Paris
AGS 1945–1949
Livres Américains
1958
F Offset 60 × 30

11 Kurt Hauert (*1924)
Basel
AGS 1952–1956
Das Basler Gewerbe an der Arbeit
Basel Craft at Work
1959
CH Linolschnitt, Buchdruck
127 × 90

12 Nelly Rudin (*1928)
Uitikon/Zürich und S-chanf
AGS 1945–1950
Saffa 1958 Zürich
1958
CH Offset 127 × 90

13 Dorothea Hofmann (*1925)
Luzern
AGS 1949–1954
Georges Méliès/Beginn der Filmkunst
Beginning of Film Art/
Gewerbemuseum Basel
1963
CH Offset 127 × 90

14 Inge H. Druckrey (*1940)
Philadelphia
AGS 1960–1965
Werbeagentur Erwin Halpern, Zürich
Orta/immer frisch/erfrischt immer
Orta/always fresh/always refreshes
1965
CH Siebdruck 127 × 90

15 Peter Olpe (*1949)
Basel
AGS 1966–1970
26. Gesellschaftsausstellung der schweizerischen Malerinnen, Bildhauerinnen und Kunstgewerblerinnen

Exhibition by the Society of Swiss Female Painters, Sculptors and Applied Artists/Kunsthalle and Gewerbemuseum Basel
1968
CH Offset 127 × 90

16 Gerhard Forster (1937–1986)
AGS 1957–1961
Foto: Ugo Mulas
Pirelli/Sempione spalla di sicurezza – Sicherheitsreifen – Safety Tyres
ca. 1967
IT Offset 68 × 48,5

17 Fridolin Müller (*1926)
Stein am Rhein
AGS 1946–1950
Messer Gabel Löffel
Knife Fork Spoon/
Kunstgewerbemuseum Zürich
Foto: Marlene Gruber
1964
CH Offset 127 × 90

18 Peter von Arx (*1937)
Basel
AGS 1957–1961
Foto: Manfred Maier
1966
Helft Brände verhüten
Help to Prevent Fires
CH Offset 127 × 90

19 Fredy Prack (*1940)
Basel
AGS 1956–1961
6. Eidg. Harmonika Musikfest
6th National Harmonica Music Festival
1971
CH Offset 127 × 90

20 Willi Wermelinger (*1933)
Geroldswil
AGS 1949–1953
Garantiert frisch! Dänische Eier!
Guaranteed Fresh! Danish Eggs!
Foto: Max Buchmann
1962
CH Offset 128 × 90,5

21 Christoph Aeppli (*1927)
Basel
AGS 1945–1949
Foto: Atelier Moeschlin
Sorgenlos in der SBB
Carefree with SBB
1969
CH Offset 1969

22 Dan Friedman (1945–1995)
AGS 1968–1970
The Yale Symphony Orchestra/
Beethoven Brahms Wagner
1973
US Siebdruck 65 × 50,5

23 Dennis Y. Ichiyama (*1944)
West Lafayette
AGS 1975–1978
Work in Progresse 79/Illinois
Arts Week
1979
US Offset 56 x 43

24 Philip C. Burton (*1946)
Chicago
AGS 1970–1975
Trans-Europ-Express/die Städte-
schnellzüge Europas
Europe's Inter-City Expresses
1970
CH Buchdruck 62 × 46

25 Ulrich Schierle (* 1935)
Bottmingen
AGS 1958–1962
50 Jahre Hockey Nordstern Basel
50 Years of Hockey Nordstern
Basel
1973
CH Offset 84 × 59,5

26 Jörg Hamburger (*1935)
Zürich
AGS 1950–1955
Juni-Festwochen 1970
1970 June Festival/
Schauspielhaus Zürich
1970
CH Offset 1278 × 90

27 Laurence Bach (*1947)
Philadelphia
AGS 1969/70
Philadelphia College of Art/
Pre-College Program
1973
US Offset 79 × 57,5

28 Jean-Benoît Lévy (*1959)
Basel
AGS 1978–1983
L'Adresse Coiffure
1988
CH Siebdruck 128 × 90,5

29 Kenneth Hiebert (*1930)
Elkins Park
AGS 1959–1964
Many Gifts, One Spirit
Foto: Kenneth Hiebert
1982
US Offset 88 × 60

30 Pierre Mendell (*1929)
München
AGS 1958–1961
Kieler Woche
Kiel Week
Mendell & Oberer, München
Foto: Hans Döring
1986
DE Offset 119 × 84

31 Reinhart Morscher (*1938)
Bern
AGS 1959–1963
Raffeln/zyliss
1981
CH Offset 128 × 90,5

32 April Greiman (*1948)
Los Angeles
AGS 1970/71
The Modern Poster/Museum of
Modern Art New York
1988
US Offset 99 × 62

33 Gregory Vines (*1946)
Basel
AGS 1972–1976
Wider besseres Wissen
Against Better Judgement/
Museum für Gestaltung Basel
1988
CH Offset 128 × 90,5

34 Robert Probst (*1951)
Cincinnati
AGS 1972–1974
From Table to Tablescape/
Formica Corporation
1990
US Offset 56 × 43

35 Anne Hoffmann (*1944)
Basel
AGS 1979–1984
Weltgeschichten – World Stories/
Museum für Gestaltung Zürich
1989
CH Siebdruck 128 × 90,5

36 Klaus Oberer (*1937), Pura
AGS 1955–1959
Die Neue Sammlung,
Arne Jacobsen
Mendell & Oberer, München
Foto: Klaus Oberer
1994
DE Offset 119 × 84

37 Steff Geissbuhler (*1942),
New York
AGS 1958–1964
AIGA/Competitions & Exhibitions
2000
US Inkjet print 89 × 61

38 Rudi Meyer (*1943), Paris
AGS 1959–1963
Giselle/Théâtre du Châtelet Paris
2001
FR Offset 150 × 100

39 Hans-Ulrich Allemann (*1944),
Philadelphia
AGS 1960–1965
Vote/USA 2000
2000
US Offset 68,5 × 40,5

40 Hans Tanner (*1957), Zürich
AGS 1981–1985
Weber, Hodel, Schmid, Zürich
Relax! Zürich Versicherungs-
Gesellschaft
1998
CH Offset 170 × 118

41 William Longhauser (*1947)
Los Angeles
Greenberg/AIGA U. Arts Lecture
Foto: Ryszard Horowitz
1994
US Offset 96,5 × 63,5

42 Georg Staehelin (*1942)
Ottenbach/Zürich
AGS 1958–1963
Netto/Nichts als Inhalt
Net/Nothing but Content/
Museum für Gestaltung Basel
1994
CH Siebdruck 128 × 90,5

Fotos/Photos:
Max Mathys, S. 45, S.55

Publikationen von Armin Hofmann (Auswahl)
Publications by Armin Hofmann (Selection)

«Plakate der Graphikklasse der Allgemeinen Gewerbeschule Basel», in: Form und Technik, Nr. 7, München 1954.

«Ein Beitrag zur formalen Erziehung des Gebrauchsgrafikers/A Contribution to the Education of the Commercial Artist», in: Graphis, Nr. 80, Zürich, November/Dezember 1958.

«Integrale Typografie, Grundprobleme des gestalterischen Schaffens», in: Typografische Monatsblätter, Sondernummer Nr. 6/7, St. Gallen 1959.

Methodik der Form- und Bildgestaltung. Aufbau, Synthese, Anwendung/Teufen 1965 (Dreisprachige Ausgabe in Deutsch, Französisch und Englisch) [New York 1965, Tokyo 1968].

«Der Weiterbildungskurs für Graphische Gestaltung an der Kunstgewerbeschule Basel», in: Graphis, Nr. 146, Zürich 1969/1970.

Armin Hofmann u. a., «Kunstgewerbeschule Basel», in: Graphis, Bd. 25, Nr. 146, Zürich 1970.

«Anregungen zum Thema konzeptionelles Entwerfen/Some Suggestions on the Subject of Conceptional Design», in: Novum Gebrauchsgraphik/Novum Education, Nr. 11, München, November 1970.

Armin Hofmann, Josef Albers, Norman Ives, Selection of Silkscreens, New Haven 1973.

«Herbert Matter, ein Rückblick/A Retrospective», in: Graphis, Nr. 212, Zürich 1981.

«Gedanken zum Plakat», in: Gewerbemuseum Basel, 30 Jahre Plakatkunst, Einfluss und Ausstrahlung der Fachklasse für Grafik AGS Basel, Basel 1983.

«Thougts on the Poster», in: Dawn Ades, The 20th Century Poster, Design of the Avantgarde, New York 1984.

«Thoughts on the Study and Making of Visual Signs, Basle School of Design/Yale School of Art, 1947 to 1985», in: Design Quarterly 130, Cambridge Mass./London 1985.

«Thoughts on the Poster», in: The Basel School of Design and Its Philosophy: The Armin Hofmann Years, 1946–1986, Goldie Paley Gallery, Moore College of Art, 1986.

Foreword, in: Kenneth J. Hiebert, Graphic Design Sources, New Haven, London 1998.

«nelly rudin. Der Übergang von der angewandten zur freien künstlerischen Tätigkeit» (1998), in: nelly rudin, Randzonen: innen ist aussen – Bilder und Objekte, Zürich 2000.

Sekundärliteratur (Auswahl)
Secondary Literature (Selection)

Burtin, Will, «Armin Hofmann», in: Graphis, Nr. 148, Zürich 1970/71.

Friedman, Daniel, «A View: Introductory Education in Typography», in: Visible Language 7, Providence, Rhode Island 1973.

Gewerbemuseum Basel, 15 Graphiker, ehemalige Schüler der Graphik-Fachklasse an der Kunstgewerbeschule Basel zeigen Arbeiten aus der Praxis, Schriften des Gewerbemuseums Basel Nr. 3, Basel 1967.

Gewerbemuseum Basel, Graphic Design, Kunstgewerbeschule Basel, Schriften des Gewerbemuseums Basel Nr. 6, Basel 1967.

Gewerbemuseum Basel, 30 Jahre Plakatkunst, Einfluss und Ausstrahlung der Fachklasse für Grafik AGS Basel, Basel 1983.

Goldie Paley Gallery, Moore College of Art, The Basel School of Design and Its Philosophy: The Armin Hofmann Years, 1946–1986, Philadelphia, PA, 1986.

Heller, Steven, Paul Rand (Vorwort von Armin Hofmann), London 1999.

Meggs, Philip B., «Design Education: Pedagogy Versus the Real World» und «The Swiss Influence: The Old New Wave», in: AIGA Journal of Graphic Design 4, New York 1986.

Monteil, Annemarie, «Der Zeichensetzer, Das Werk und die Lehre des Grafikers Armin Hofmann», in: Basler Magazin, Nr. 47, Basel, 22. November 1997.

Müller, Rolf, «Armin Hofmann», in: High Quality, Nr. 9, München 1987.

Nelson, George, «Collaboration in Switzerland: Basel's Trade School Integrates Architecture with the Arts», in: Architectural Forum, Chicago, June 1963.

Ohchi, Hiroshi, «Armin Hofmann, Switzerland», in: Idea, Nr. 5, Tokyo 1970.

Rotzler, Willy, «Lehrer an der Schule für Gestaltung Basel», in: Willy Rotzler, Fritz Schärer, Karl Wobmann, Das Plakat in der Schweiz, Schaffhausen 1990.

Weingart, Wolfgang, «Armin Hofmann, Gestalter, Lehrer und Pädagoge/Graphic Designer and educator», in: Typografische Monatsblätter, Sonderheft, Nr. 3, Basel 1986.

Wichmann, Hans, Hg., Armin Hofmann: Werk, Erkundung, Lehre, Basel, Boston, Berlin 1989.

Steven Heller ist Art Director der New York Times Book Review and Co-Direktor des MFA/Design Programs der School of Visual Arts in New York. Er ist Autor und Herausgeber von über 80 Büchern zu Design und Alltagskultur, einschliesslich Paul Rand (Phaidon Press) und The Graphic Design Reader (Allworth Press).

Steven Heller is art director of the New York Times Book Review and coChair of the MFA/Design program at the School of Visual Arts in New York. He is the author of over 80 books on design and popular culture, including Paul Rand (Phaidon Press) and The Graphic Design Reader (Allworth Press).

DANK

Diese Publikation wäre nicht möglich gewesen ohne die grosse Hilfsbereitschaft vieler Personen. Allen voran danken wir Armin und Dorothea Hofmann für ihre liebenswürdige und geduldige Unterstützung. Für die Beschaffung von materiellen und immateriellen Informationen waren uns Ken Friedman, Andreas His, Gérard Ifert, Max Mathys, Chris Pullman, Georg Staehelin, Rolf Thalmann und Wolfgang Weingart eine grosse Hilfe. Der Aufruf an ehemalige Studierende von Armin Hofmann, eigene Plakate einzusenden, um die Plakatsammlung als Ort der Forschung und Vermittlung zu alimentieren, ist mit einer Begeisterung beantwortet worden, deren Grund wir als Respekt werten, den diese Gestalterinnen und Gestalter ihrem Lehrer noch heute entgegenbringen.

THANKS

This publication was possible only because a lot of people were willing to help. Above all we would like to thank Armin and Dorothea Hofmann for their charming and patient support. Ken Friedman, Andreas His, Gérard Ifert, Max Mathys, Chris Pullman, Georg Staehelin, Rolf Thalmann and Wolfgang Weingart gave us a great deal of assistance by providing information both material and immaterial. Our appeal to former students of Armin Hofmann to submit their own posters to feed the Poster Collection as a research and communication resource met with an enthusiasm we interpret as the respect these designers still feel for their teacher.

Eine Publikation des Museum für Gestaltung Zürich
Christian Brändle, Direktor

A Publication of the Museum für Gestaltung Zürich
Christian Brändle, Director

Armin Hofmann
Konzept, Redaktion/Concept, Editing:
Felix Studinka, Christina Reble
Lektorat/Sub-editing: Mark Welzel
Übersetzung/Translation:
Wolfgang Himmelberg, Michael Robinson
Gestaltung/Design:
Integral Lars Müller/Hendrik Schwantes
Lithografie/Repro: Seelitho AG, CH-Gossau
Druck, Einband/Printing, binding: Kösel,
Altusried-Krugzell, Germany

Reihe/«Poster Collection» Series
Herausgegeben von/Edited by
Museum für Gestaltung Zürich, Plakatsammlung
Bettina Richter, Kuratorin der Plakatsammlung/
Curator of the Poster Collection
In Zusammenarbeit mit/In cooperation with
Mirjam Fischer, Publikationen/
Publications Museum für Gestaltung Zürich

 hdk

—
Zürcher Hochschule der Künste
Zurich University of the Arts

Museum für Gestaltung Zürich
CH-8005 Zürich/Switzerland
www.museum-gestaltung.ch
www.eMuseum.ch

Museum für Gestaltung Zürich
Plakatsammlung/Poster Collection
CH-8005 Zürich/Switzerland
sammlungen@museum-gestaltung.ch

Lars Müller Publishers
CH-8005 Zürich/Switzerland
books@lars-muller.ch
www.lars-mueller-publishers.com

ISBN 978-3-03778-004-6
Erste Auflage/First Edition 2003

Printed in Germany

Wir danken für die Unterstützung/
For their support we thank: